This book is dedicated to Bob Cieslukowski
whose passion for grouse and generosity made it possible.

Acknowledgements

I would like to thank Bob Cieslukowski, without whom this book would not have been possible, the many people who helped me with this project, giving their time and knowledge unreservedly; without their dedication and enthusiam the rich diversity of the uplands would be lost to us all.

Lastly my wife, Monique. I cannot thank her enough for the help, encouragement and support she has given me in producing this book.

The author and publishers have made every effort to ensure the accuracy of the information in this book at the time of going to press. However, they cannot accept any responsibility for any loss, injury or inconvenience resulting from the use of information contained in this book.

© Simon Gudgeon 2001

ISBN 0 9526380 4 5

British Library Cataloguing in Publication Data. A catalogue record for this book is available from the British Library.

Designed and published by Ptarmigan Publishing Limited, Devizes, Wiltshire
Reprographics and print by Raithby, Lawrence & Company Ltd, Leicester

A PASSION FOR
GROUSE

AN ARTIST'S AND SPORTSMAN'S VIEW

SIMON GUDGEON

edited by Mike Barnes

Flying Grouse: bronze. Edition of 12.

Simon Gudgeon

CONTENTS

The heather uplands of Great Britain are unique. The combined influence of latitude, Gulf Stream and height above sea level has created a rich habitat for an exceptionally wide diversity of flora and fauna. It is also a wilderness which has a particular attraction for conservationists, walkers, climbers, sportsmen and, of course, artists. It may seem as if these groups had conflicting interests and agendas, but they all share a passion for these uplands, and they are all equally concerned to protect them for future generations.

In this remarkable book, Simon Gudgeon has translated this passion into words and pictures, which vividly capture the enduring quality of the special landscape of the heather uplands. I am sure that his book will give immense pleasure to all who value this wonderful piece of our national heritage.

THE RED GROUSE

INTRODUCTION

I shot the first grouse I ever saw. It was not done in any great style, I was so daunted by its speed, as it flew towards my butt, I was practically mesmerised, eventually bringing it down with a late, late second barrel. It was a moment I will never forget and was the beginning of a passion for grouse that has been with me ever since. In the intervening years I have spent many happy hours on the moor, mostly without a gun and in all seasons and all weather. In that time the allure of this, the king of gamebirds, has intensified as my knowledge of the bird and habitat increased. This book is an attempt to increase the understanding of this unique bird and show that the conservation of moorland for grouse is of benefit to all the birds, mammals, insects, wild flowers, mosses and other flora that share its habitat. It is by no means a definitive work, that would have taken several volumes of closely worded text, but an attempt to fire your enthusiasm to learn more. Nothing you read in this book will improve your shooting, however, a greater understanding could perhaps in some way encourage a wider appreciation of grouse and the environment in which this wonderful bird lives.

A YEAR ON THE MOOR

Rather than dealing with the behaviour, breeding and diet of the red grouse separately I feel it will give a better insight into the lifestyle of this unique bird if we follow it through the course of a year. Although the timing of our year is governed by the months, that of the grouse is determined by the weather, the food supply, and, most of all, the urge to survive and procreate. It is virtually impossible to say, with any degree of certainty, what a grouse will be doing at any particular time of year as this will depend, more than anything else, upon the weather. Although conditions will affect its behaviour, the grouse is a very hardy little bird, superbly adapted to its environment, and it will, if healthy, live through the most severe of climatic conditions so long as the food supply is not affected.

AUTUMN

It's October and, except in years of plenty, most of the shooting will have come to an end, allowing the cock birds to establish their territories with the minimum of interference. Although when most of us visit the moor during the shooting season grouse congregate in coveys or packs they are essentially a territorial bird and once their brood has become independent they will want to revert to their territorial behaviour. Older cock grouse will often start to re-establish their territories in October, or earlier. Anyone who has been on a grouse moor in August will have witnessed the territorial display of the cock grouse, where he flies steeply from the ground making a series of loud barking 'aa' calls, and then descends with rapidly beating wings, neck extended, and tail fanned, and a slowing 'ka ka ka' call. It is, like the call of the curlew, one of the most memorable and stirring sounds of the moor. Last year's cock bird will often return to the previous year's territory and will allow their male offspring to establish territories around him, even allowing them to encroach onto his territory. By doing this he will give his offspring a better chance to inherit his territory should he not survive.

The most sought after territories are those which contain a diversity of habitat, such as patches of different aged heather, other edible vegetation, and water. A large rock or stone wall, upon which the cock grouse can survey his territory and see intruders is also an advantage. It will be between 2 and 30 acres in size, depending upon the quality of the habitat. The type of underlying rock will affect the soil fertility and the nutritional quality of the heather which will be a determining factor when the grouse decides upon the size of his territory. In areas where the underlying rock is granite, as in much of Scotland, the soil fertility is low, the same applies to areas of thick peat, whereas areas where the underlying rock is limestone will have greater soil fertility and will be able to sustain much smaller territories and carry a higher population of grouse. The supply of a nutrient rich food source is especially important to the female when she is producing eggs and building up strength before brooding.

As winter progresses the grouse will fluctuate between being on their territories, normally in the early morning, and congregating in large packs. Packing is especially prevalent in times of harsh weather when territories are totally abandoned as grouse search for food that has survived the effects of frost and cold. During extreme weather, when the ground is covered with snow, grouse can be forced off the hill entirely in search for food. They have been seen eating the buds of birch and hawthorn, and rowan berries. In past times when oats were stooked in the field after harvest grouse were regular visitors and during a particularly bad winter in 1894 there are accounts of them feeding in a turnip field.

Unless grouse are forced off the hill by extreme weather their diet is almost exclusively heather during the winter months and because they have to consume it in greater bulk, it is crucial that the moor has a plentiful supply of short or close heather to carry them through the winter. The majority of the moor is covered with brown winter heather and looks, on a wet day, very bleak and drab. Grouse search out the fresh green heather on the lower branches of the plant sheltered from the frost and cold. These green shoots are more nutritious and are found on short heather which is more plentiful on a well burnt moor. Older heather tends to become more open as it grows and is of little value as a food source. Bilberry leaves and stalks,

when available, will also form part of the winter diet and are a valuable commodity that should be encouraged on a moor. As the nutritional value of the heather is lower in winter, and because the brown winter heather makes up part of their diet, grouse have to eat a greater bulk of food to maintain condition. This can be up to five times more than in the summer months.

If, during November, December, and January, the weather becomes milder then the packs will disperse and territories will be resumed. The grouse will often pair up at this time, sometimes resuming the pair bond from the previous year, however, as soon as the harsh weather returns they will once again congregate in packs.

From February, weather permitting, the grouse will start to prepare for breeding, the cock birds vigorously defending their territories, with fights, sometimes serious, breaking out amongst rival males, for a good territory almost certainly guarantees a mate and increases the chances of breeding success. This defence of territory is not just directed against other grouse, particularly aggressive males will even attack hill walkers venturing onto their area. In view of the growing 'Right to Roam' lobby this type of behaviour is to be encouraged! Where the grouse are plentiful older birds forced off their territory and young birds that have failed to establish themselves are relegated onto the more marginal areas of moorland. Generally, these birds fail to establish a territory because they are weaker, either through disease or being a late brood, and so suffer from a higher mortality rate than the territorial grouse.

March is also the time when they begin to pair in earnest. The dramatic territorial display of the cock grouse, described earlier, is also used as an amorous demonstration of his vigour. This can lead to neighbouring cocks responding and, in a testosterone induced chain reaction, other grouse will join in across the moor. The females, who are particularly attracted to this type of display, can often be seen flying around the moor in small packs, alighting on different territories to cast a critical eye over the area and its incumbent. If he is satisfactory on all counts a female will adopt a submissive posture and the male, with red combs above the eye fully erect, will strut about with wings drooped and tail fanned in a courtship display.

Once the pair has become established the happy couple will remain on their territory, with the male being ever vigilant for intruders and jealously guarding the female and making sure that she does not leave. When they fly around together the male will be on the outside to keep her within the boundary of the territory, even to the extent of bumping into her in mid air. The time between pairing and egg laying is critical for the hen grouse, as she must build up her reserves at the end of a hard winter to enable her to survive incubating the eggs. This period coincides with the emergence of buds on the cotton grass which provide a highly nutritious source of protein and the hen will consume all she can. Unfortunately as the cotton grass is the most sought after food on the moor, there is strong competition from sheep and deer which may have an influence on egg and chick production.

The nest is usually built on dry ground in thick heather on the edge of a burnt patch so providing cover as well as visibility. It will be sited reasonably close to a source of grit, an area where the newly hatched chicks can feed and water. This latter point is important when trying to improve grouse densities on a dry moor as the wet areas and bog flushes provide an abundant source of insect life for the grouse chicks. I visited a moor in Yorkshire where the keeper had dug small dew ponds all over the moor. If there was no spring nearby or no method of retaining water he would line

them with concrete, thus when the chicks hatched the hen did not have far to travel to let them feed and drink. A grouse will take her chicks up to 500 yards in search of insects, which for a small grouse chick over rough ground is a mammoth task. The supply of small ponds will help reduce mortality by not exposing them to predation and bad weather, and also not expending energy when food sources are scarce, as in a cold spring.

A slight hollow is scraped out and lined with heather and grass in which the hen will lay a clutch of between 6 and 10 eggs. In cold, wet springs the number may well be less and if the hen is suffering from disease it can be as few as two. The eggs are usually laid from late April into early May, although in this, as in most factors to do with grouse behaviour, the weather plays an important role, and in mild years eggs have been found as early as March. The level of the moor above sea level will also play a role as the higher moors will be colder and egg laying and hatching will be delayed.

Yet while weather plays a crucial role in the breeding success of grouse, it is probably not as crucial as the condition of the hen when she begins to lay. Her condition will determine egg numbers and fertility. The hen will lay one egg every twenty four hours and even though she will cover the eggs with vegetation in between, a hard frost at this time can damage the eggs before she has started sitting. However, there have been recorded instances where the frost was so hard that the eggs were frozen to the nest and each other and yet they still hatched successfully. A hen grouse is a tenacious little bird, especially when nesting, and she will stay on her nest through most types of weather, even through heavy snowstorms when she can be completely covered by snow, not leaving the nest for days on end, even to feed, in case the eggs become chilled Heavy rain is the greatest threat as it can, if it persists for long enough, waterlog the nest which will cause her to abandon the eggs permanently. If she can avoid all these pitfalls it will take about 22 days for the eggs to hatch. During this time the cock grouse stays close by and escorts the hen when she briefly leaves the nest for feeding. Towards the end of May, when the chicks begin to hatch, moor owners and keen shots alike will avidly watch the weather forecasts, hoping for fine weather to give the chicks a good start.

Warm weather is ideal during hatching, though intermittent rain is necessary to produce the insect life upon which the young grouse will feed. The chicks leave the nest soon after emerging from the egg and the hen will take them in search of food and water. Their main diet for the first ten days of their life is insects which are protein rich and it is critical that they have an abundant supply. The chicks will eat young heather shoots on newly burnt areas as well but they cannot survive on heather alone so cold weather at this time can cause a great

deal of harm. Both parents take part in caring for the brood although it is the hen that seems to be more actively involved in their protection. If disturbed she will feign a broken wing and pathetically try to lure the intruder away from her brood. If you witness this behaviour you should try and leave the area as the chicks will remain motionless and almost invisible, and are easily trodden on. The cock grouse's main role seems to be watching over the hen and her brood and warning of any danger. However, at this time the hen is at her weakest, the egg laying and brooding having sapped her strength, and therefore any harsh weather will not only take its toll on the young but also may kill the hen. Should this occur, or any other disaster befall the hen, the cock grouse will take over the rearing of the brood, even if newly hatched, and successfully rear the young.

Young grouse grow rapidly, being able to fly at two weeks old and are fully grown at just over a month. This rapid growth would seem to be a way of overcoming the adversities they face as they mature, for although an adult grouse will, if healthy, happily survive the most extreme weather, their young cannot. Heavy rain, snow, or frost can all occur on the moor during early summer when the chicks are at their most vulnerable, one of the most dangerous periods is before they are fully grown but are too large to be brooded and protected from the weather by the hen.

Their diet will change after about three weeks and contain more and more heather. To help them extract the nutrients from this fibrous diet they collect grit in their gizzard which helps grind down the heather before it enters the intestine. During the summer months other plant species will supplement the diet of heather as the grouse build up strength during the short summer. These plants can form up to 50 % of their summer diet. They will feed intermittently throughout the day, resting and dusting in between searching for food. In the evening they will feed hard to provide enough sustenance to get them through the night, although in northern parts this will only be a few hours long when, once again, just before dawn the moor will begin to wake up, and grouse will start calling to one another as they start their day. This is a magical moment. Sitting in the heather listening to the grouse call as the sky brightens from the east. If you have the opportunity to experience it don't turn it down.

The family group will remain together well into the autumn, forming the coveys that fly through the line of butts on the glorious twelfth. It does not take long before the coveys start to merge into large packs, up to several hundred in size in a good year, all the while becoming wilder and more wary. It is these later grouse that are truly sporting.

THE FLIGHT OF THE GROUSE

When grouse start coming towards the butts, seemingly appearing from nowhere, an explosion of birds jinking and turning in the wind, the excitment is intense. Driven grouse are a uniquely testing bird and, for me, the ultimate in driven shooting. The speed and agility of grouse are astounding. They are, after all, a ground dwelling bird that spends little time on the wing. Yet they can fly at over 60 miles per hour and change course with a flick of the tail, sometimes banking so hard that they are almost on their backs.

The flight of the grouse is fascinating and I could spend hours sitting at the side of a butt, during a drive, watching them fly. The perception of flight is very different from when you are shooting. Then there is little time to watch the grouse and absorb the movement, which is perhaps why most grouse paintings have the grouse coming towards the viewer with wings set as though gliding. When I first started painting these magnificent birds mine were the same, but as I spent more time watching them I started painting them with different wing beats. Some that had their wings up high ready for the downward beat, others that had reached the extreme of the down beat, and some in mid-wing beat.

Many people, observing these paintings, commented that they had never seen grouse flying like that and then I realised that when shooting one is focusing on a target and all of one's concentration is devoted to judging distance, speed and lead. The mind does not absorb the movement of the grouse. It is too busy, and so when you are off the moor and see a painting of a covey of grouse gliding you think that is how they fly. Grouse cannot travel the distances they do, at speeds of nearly sixty miles an hour, sometimes into the wind, with their wings in the gliding position all the time. They have to beat them for speed and manoeuverablity. The only way to see this is to take time off shooting and sit in the heather during a drive. Pick one bird out of a covey and watch it as it flies past the butts, you will be amazed by their movement. On warm days, or when they have been flying some distance, they will also fly with their beaks open in order to get sufficient oxygen, which, if you think about it, is obvious, as we humans tend to breath through our mouth if we run.

The other misconception that probably originated with early paintings of grouse in flight was the length of their wings. Look at early work of Archibald Thorburn or George Edward Lodge and the wings of the grouse flying towards the viewer are tiny. I am not trying to disparage these artists; Thorburn was, in my view, the greatest sporting artist of all time, with Lodge and Harrison not far behind. However they did paint the wings of a grouse too short, whilst gliding the wingspan will be about 50% more than the length of the body. So for a hen grouse measuring 14 inches the wingspan will be about 21 inches. If the bird banks to change direction and fully extends its wings this can increase by 4-6 inches. Next time you pick up a dead grouse spread its wings and just look at the length.

GROUSE DISEASE

THE STRONGYLE WORM

A friend who is trying to restore an overgrazed moor in Yorkshire has, as his motto, *pessimus inimicus ovis alius ovis est* - the worst enemy of a sheep is another sheep. This could neatly be changed to *pessimus inimicus lagopus alius lagopus est* - the worst enemy of a grouse is another grouse. Others may wish to give this accolade to the fox, or the hen harrier. Nonetheless, when it comes to one of the most frequently discussed topics in grouse moor management, namely the strongyle worm, a grouse's worst enemy is another grouse as they spread this parasitic nematode with sometimes catastrophic results.

The life cycle of the worm begins as an egg laid in the caeca gut by the adult worm. The grouse has two caecum leading off from the small intestine, they both come to a dead end and so are frequently referred to as the blind gut. This is where the grouse digests the heather that has been broken down by the grit in its gizzard. The eggs pass out of the host grouse through droppings. Grouse have two types of droppings - the tube shaped fibrous ones, with a white tip at the end (commonly seen in small piles dotted around the moor),

and the brown viscous droppings that can best be described, and I do not mean to repel you from a favourite dessert, as melted chocolate mousse. It is in the latter, deposited once a day, that the eggs emerge from the grouse and develop within the droppings, moulting twice before emerging as an infective larvae.

The larvae, using the thin water film around the heather plant, climbs up towards the growing tip and, once there, develops a tough sheath to protect it from the weather until a grouse eats the heather and so swallows the infective larvae. The parasite then makes its way to one of the blind guts and develops into the adult worm which burrows into the gut wall where it will mate, lay eggs and start the process again. I find it fascinating that a small brainless worm that is little more than 6mm long, and thinner than a hair, is able to achieve this. How does it know that it has to climb to the top of the heather? How is it able to find its way to the blind gut? After all, if it misses the turning, it's back into daylight. Any number of mistakes could be made in the whole process yet with monotonous regularity the

THE GROUSE INGESTS
THE INFECTIVE LARVAE
WHILST EATING HEATHER.

ADULT WORMS LIVE
IN THE GROUSE'S
CAECA.

THE WORMS LAY EGGS
WHICH PASS OUT IN
THE GROUSE'S
FAECES

THE LARVAE CLIMBS
UP THE HEATHER.

THE EGGS HATCH

3RD STAGE LARVAE

YOUNG EMBRYO

TWO MOULTS

larvae get it right and, when the worm burden is high enough, kill their host which in turn leads to their own demise.

In times of high grouse population the worms reproduce and spread rapidly which leads to the boom/bust cycle experienced by so many moors. The weather, though, can help or hinder the development of the worm. During very hot spells the larvae can become entombed in the droppings as a hard crust forms, this type of weather also means that there is no thin film of water on the heather to facilitate the larvae's progress up the plant. What they require are warm damp conditions which is why the extreme boom/bust cycles seem to affect the wet moors rather than the dry ones. The wettish moors also have better conditions to produce big grouse numbers which exacerbates the problem. Warm damp weather is also ideal for the heather beetle so that at the bottom of the cycle, when the grouse are suffering from high worm burdens, they may also have to contend with a reduced food supply due to the degradation of the beetle. The combination of the two can affect the long-term viability of a moor and lead to its demise.

The strongyle worm affects the condition of the grouse by burrowing into the gut wall causing internal bleeding and, as the caecal gut is where many of the nutrients are extracted from the grouse's diet, they reduce its digestive efficiency. It does, however, take several thousand worms to cause a loss of condition, although once the number is over 7,000 it does not bode well for the grouse. As the worm count increases the grouse becomes weaker, which is why birds that are suffering from a high count are often found lower down on the hill as they no longer have the strength to fly back to the high ground. They are also more susceptible to mammalian predation. Dead birds will have emaciated breast muscles and their caeca will be swollen with bloody debris.

There are two critical times when the grouse become infected with the worm, the first being in late summer when all the larvae eaten will develop into adult worms. Later in the year the larvae entering the caeca gut will remain in a state of arrested development until the following spring when they will develop into adult worms. This is the second critical period as not only are the larvae inside the gut developing but also the larvae which have over-wintered in the droppings will respond to the warmer temperatures and develop into infective larvae. Unfortunately this period coincides with the hen grouse trying to improve her condition to enable her to produce eggs and give her the strength to incubate them. In times of high worm count this is when the highest mortality will occur with the hen sometimes just dying on her nest or brood.

SIMON GUDGEON

Worm counts in grouse are a much discussed topic, especially during the shooting season, as the worm burden will give an indication of how hard the grouse should be shot. If the burden is high then the population should be reduced, especially the older birds as they carry a higher number of worms. If low, the birds should be in good condition the following spring and, weather permitting, should breed well, so more grouse should be left to boost numbers the following year. Further worm counts can be carried out in pre-breeding birds in spring to assess their condition after the winter, although this is only possible if dead birds are found after road kills or fence strikes. This will give an indication of their breeding condition and thus an early idea of the breeding potential of the moor.

The practicalities of counting the worms in a grouse are relatively simple and do not need masses of equipment or laboratory conditions. You will need :
*Two sieves, one with a very fine mesh
    and the other slightly coarser
    (212um and 810um mesh)
A pair of dissecting scissors
300ml measuring cylinder
Petri dish
A bright lamp
A high sided washing tray
    (photographic type)
15ml syringe
500ml glass beaker.*

Place the larger mesh sieve on top of the fine one and put in the sink. The overflow pipe should allow the water in the sink to be slightly lower than the top sieve. Remove the gut from the grouse and gently tease them apart to locate the caeca or blind gut. Take one of them and separate it from the small intestine. Carefully insert one blade of the scissors into the caecum and cut along its length and then cut it up into three or four equal lengths and place it in the top sieve. Gently let the water from the tap flow over the gut for about ten minutes, cleaning them and flushing all the worms into the lower sieve where they will be trapped by the fine mesh.

Take the lower sieve and place it upside down in the photographic tray and wash out the contents with 300 ml of water so that the trapped worms will end up in the tray with the water. Empty the tray into the 500ml beaker and stir to ensure that the worms are evenly distributed then use the syringe to remove 10ml of water and empty into a petri dish. Place the petri dish onto a dark surface, a black tile is ideal especially if you etch a grid onto it with 1cm gaps, and, shining the lamp down onto the dish, you will be able to spot the tiny worms. Using the grid on the tile it is easier to count the worms, some of which will be broken so only count ones that are more than half the average length of a whole worm.

Repeat the above until you have a total of three samples and add all three counts together and multiply by ten. This will give you the number of worms from the one gut, i.e. 30ml of samples from the 300ml used to wash out the sieve, then if you multiply that by two you will have the total worm count for both the caecum. Thus if the three samples had counts of 27, 29, & 25 the calculation would be 81 x 10 x 2 = 1620, which is not too serious.

It is advisable to sample several birds at a time to give you an idea of the worm burden per bird throughout the moor. However a simple average of the counts for each bird will give a distorted picture as there will be some birds with a very high burden and the majority with a lower one. So a geometric mean, calculated using logarithms (I knew that all those years of studying O level maths would one day prove useful) gives a more accurate worm burden as it reduces the bias introduced by one large count.

	Actual worm count	Logarithm of worm count	Action on calculator
Bird 1	1060	3.025	1060 "Log"
Bird 2	2030	3.307	2030 "Log"
Bird 3	3750	3.574	3750 "Log"
Bird 4	960	2.982	960 "Log"
Bird 5	8080	3.907	8080 "Log"
Number of birds	5	5	5
Arithmetic mean	3176	3.359	(Birds 1+2+3+4+5)/5
Geometric mean		2287	Anti-log (10*)

A worked example for calculating geometric average worm burdens – the corrected average. Here we take the average of 5 different worm counts. Note that the true average calculated with logarithms is less than the average calculated using the normal arithmetic procedure. The geometric calculation reduces the biases introduced by one large count.

No one has yet been able to totally eradicate the disease, and I am not sure that would be a good idea anyway, though all is not doom and gloom as there are a number of weapons that can be used to combat the most severe effects of the disease. In order to digest heather, grouse keep a supply of coarse grit in their gizzards which they use to grind down the tough fibrous plant before it goes to the blind guts where the nutrients are extracted. Most keepers deploy large quantities of Cornish quartz grit around the moor, with a number of small piles in each grouse's territory, so there is a ready supply for them. Through the use of medicated grit it is possible to, not only help the bird's digestion, but also reduce the impact of the worm by killing some of them, reduce the egg production of the surviving worms and also reduce the development of the infective larvae within the blind gut.

Medicated grit is just like ordinary grit with a coating of fat that incorporates an anthelmintic drug. This makes it resistant to the effects of water and sunlight so remaining effective for several months. It is placed in small piles, preferably on areas of burnt heather or other accessible areas, about 250 metres apart so there will several piles within each grouse territory. To ensure that shot grouse are not carrying the active drug the medicated grit should only be placed on the moor from after the end of shooting until April. This will allow the warm summer weather to break down the active ingredients in the drug before August 12th, and the birds themselves will lose all traces of the drug before the start of the season.

Although medicated grit will not eradicate the worm burden in a grouse it will reduce its impact, especially in the brooding hens and young grouse. Trials carried out by the Game Conservancy Trust have shown that there was no difference in clutch size between the hens that had access to medicated grit and those that did not. However chick survival was significantly improved with those on medicated grit rearing between 1.5 and three extra chicks per hen.

The other method that can be used to control the worm is by direct dosing where the grouse are caught at night, using a lamp and a net, and then a small tube is inserted down their throat and 2ml of an anthelmintic drug is administered orally. This arduous task is undertaken by the keepers working in teams of two or three throughout the winter, from the end of the shooting season until mid April. The nights need to be dark with no moon and no rain or snow and walking along the moor it is easy to pick out the reflection from the eye of the grouse. Although at this time of year the grouse are often found in packs during the day, by nightfall

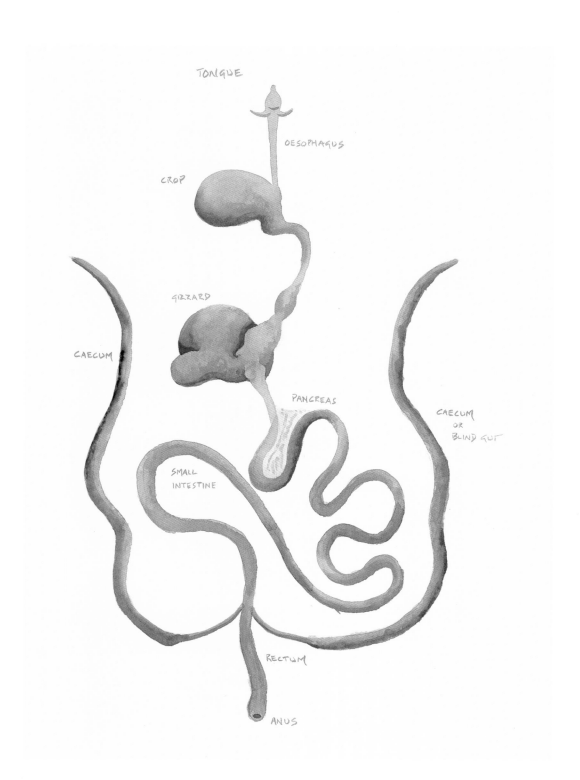

TONGUE

OESOPHAGUS

CROP

GIZZARD

CAECUM

PANCREAS

CAECUM OR BLIND GUT

SMALL INTESTINE

RECTUM

ANUS

they will usually have returned to their territories in pairs, with the cock and the hen within a few yards of each other. The first to be spotted is usually the cock as the hen will be crouching lower in the heather. However it is the hen that must be caught first, as it is more important to dose her to improve her strength for breeding. Also, if the cock is caught first the hen will take flight whereas if it is the other way round the cock will often run towards the captors to defend his mate. Working in pairs a team can, depending on the terrain, dose 40-100 birds per night and each bird will be tagged, and a record kept, so that it is not dosed again another night. In practice this would not often occur as the keepers tend to know their grouse territories and do not cover the same piece of ground twice.

The immediate effect of dosing is the total eradication of all worms in the grouse's blind guts. Whilst this may seem to be the grouse managers answer to the perpetual boom/bust cycle, in practice it is not always the case for a grouse will start being reinfected as soon as it has been dosed as it picks up more infective larvae from the heather it eats. In practice these larvae will stay in a state of arrested development over the winter and so should not weaken the grouse.

Furthermore, the drug does not kill off the larvae that are in a state of arrested development within the gut at the time it is dosed, so that when spring comes, and the larvae develop into worms, the grouse can suffer from a very high worm burden. Thus the most effective time to dose is after the spring rise in worms although this leaves very little time to dose the population before they start breeding.

There is a considerable amount of debate as to the effectiveness of direct dosing with some moors showing good results and others gaining little benefit. Most agree, however, that it can prevent the severe crashes in the grouse population in years when there is a high worm burden. There is a danger, however, that grouse moor managers will use direct dosing, which is extremely time consuming, to maintain their grouse stocks at the expense of good moorland management techniques and keepering. This is why I feel that an effective cure for the strongyle worm would be a disaster for grouse as it would lead to shortcuts being taken in other areas of moorland management. The red grouse is, after all, the only truly wild gamebird that is shot in any number in the Great Britain, and this is only possible by maintaining their habitat.

The other major disease that grouse suffer from is louping ill which is spread by ticks, a small relative of the spider that lives on a diet of blood which is sucked from the host. Whilst little more than a nuisance to most species they live off, they can spread louping ill which will often prove fatal for grouse and, to a lesser extent, sheep.

Louping ill is a virus that attacks the central nervous system causing the sufferer to stagger or 'loup', eventually being unable to walk. It can prove fatal in 10%-60% of sheep that are infected and over 80% of grouse. It is spread by the tick's saliva moving from tick to host and from host to tick.

The life cycle is fascinating consisting of four stages, egg, larvae, nymph and adult, the last three of which only feed once before moving onto the next stage of their development. Once they have fed they drop back into the vegetation and can wait a year before their next meal, so that if they survive all four stages they can be up to four years old. The larvae and nymphs will feed on both mammals and birds whilst the adult female only feeds off mammals where she will inflate her sack-like body to many times its original size as she gorges herself on blood. Each of these ticks can consume up to 2ml of blood so if the host is heavily infected it can add up to quite a large amount. The adult males do

not feed at all, instead just seeking out a female and mating whilst she is on the host. So the life cycle of the tick is very important when trying to combat this disease which can seriously affect the capital value of a moor. If there are no mammals for the adult female to feed off then she will not be able to produce eggs and the cycle will stop, which is why louping ill is rare on moor where sheep are regularly dipped and few other mammals are present on the moor. The other main host species for ticks are deer and mountain hares and, although neither of these suffer from louping ill, they can transmit it between ticks so that louping ill can persist in the absence grouse or sheep. The Game Conservancy Trust's research into louping ill found that on one estate, where mountain hares were removed over a seven year period, the tick population was reduced by 99% and the incidence of louping ill in shot grouse was down from 80% to 10% with a 400% increase in grouse density.

Although the reduction in host species may not always be possible, either for economic or conservation reasons, other methods of control can be used to reduce the incidence of the disease by reducing tick numbers. The most important of these is the treatment of sheep by vaccinating them against louping ill and treating them with an anti-tick drug that kills the ticks once they get on the sheep. The second is

the removal of the habitat favoured by ticks, and fortunately this is also the habitat that is largely useless for grouse. The bracken beds and Molinia grass provide a damp humid mat of vegetation which the ticks need to survive during their dormant period and reducing this type of habitat will not only lessen the incidence of louping ill, it will also improve the habitat for grouse and lead to increased numbers. However ticks will survive perfectly well in heather so the main attack on them should be against their mammalian hosts.

While strongyle worm and louping ill are the two major diseases that affect grouse, they may also suffer occasionally from coccidiosis, and tapeworms but their incidence is insignificant. However, a word of warning... increasingly partridge and pheasant are being released onto moors to provide additional sport and, whilst grouse only suffer from three or four diseases, reared gamebirds suffer from a huge number. It is unknown whether any of these diseases can be transmitted to grouse. If they can, once the ground is infected, it will be impossible to turn back the clock. I believe that we are exposing these wild gamebirds to an unnecessary risk for short term commercial gain and that it would be more beneficial, for the grouse, if the time and money spent on reared gamebirds was redirected into proper grouse management.

"AGEING" GROUSE

Ageing grouse is important for two reasons. Firstly, the proportion of old birds to young shows how well the breeding season has gone and the best time to make an assessment is during the July counts. Secondly, old grouse tend to be tougher than young ones and consequently their value as a table bird is lower.

From a grouse management point of view old grouse do not breed as well, and, more importantly, they also carry a larger quantity of the strongyle worm and so will increase the worm burden on a moor, thus infecting the younger, healthier grouse. So it is better to shoot the older grouse during the season to improve the health of the moor. There is very little evidence of how long grouse live in the wild, although remarkably most do not survive more than two seasons. Whilst I was researching for this book I spoke to a keeper who has been direct dosing his grouse for fourteen years, during which time he has ringed each bird whilst dosing, and kept records, so he knows the age of most of the grouse on his moor. He regularly finds grouse aged 5-6 years old and his record is a pair of grouse where the cock was 10 years old and the hen 9 years. The older birds were virtually always found furthest from the butts where the experienced birds would, year after year, turn back over the beaters and never reach the guns.

In the game larder there are several methods of assessing the age of a grouse, some more accurate than others. The commonest method is looking at the primary feathers of the bird: in a young bird the third primary will be slightly shorter than the first two. This is because the young grouse do not moult the first two primary and so, early in the season, the third primary is not fully grown. Later in the season the feather will be fully grown and so this method cannot be used.

The second method is to hold the head of the bird between your first and second finger and push your thumb into the middle of the skull. If the skull is easily depressed then it is a young bird as the skull of a young bird is softer than that of an old one. Similarly the strength of the lower leg bones can signify the birds age, with younger birds having weaker bones. Toe nail scars, too, are indicative of age. Older birds moult their toe nails each autumn and this leaves a ridge at the top of the nail closest to the foot. This is a more accurate method of assessing age later in the season, once the older birds have started to shed their toe nails.

Lastly, for those who are really keen or obsessed, an inspection of the ovaries or testes, found in the upper side of the body cavity just forward of the kidneys, will help with ageing as older birds have bigger ones.

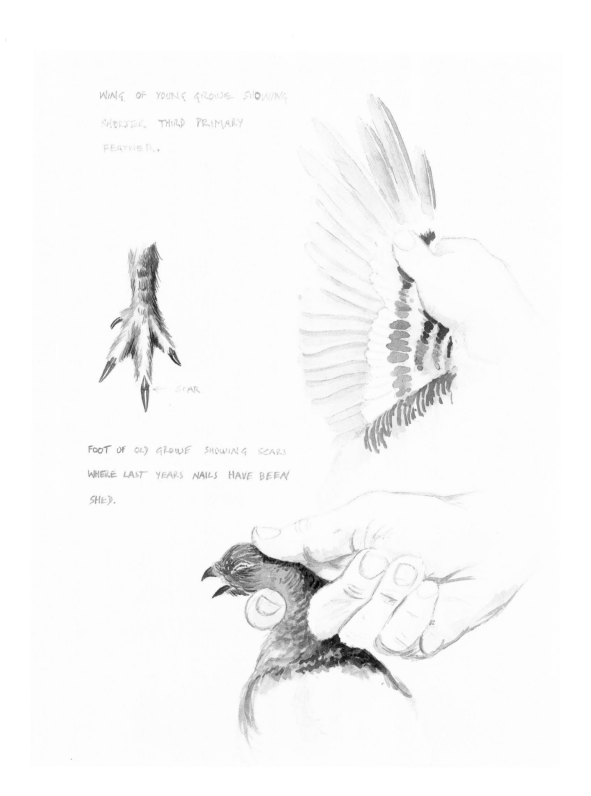

WING OF YOUNG GROUSE SHOWING
SHORTER THIRD PRIMARY
FEATHER.

← SCAR

FOOT OF OLD GROUSE SHOWING SCARS
WHERE LAST YEARS NAILS HAVE BEEN
SHED.

HABITAT

THE CREATION OF MOORLAND

Up until around 5,000 years ago most of the areas of moorland we know today were covered with trees and the small grouse population that existed would have lived on the edges of woodland above the tree line and in small clearings. It was during the Neolithic period that the influence of man began to dominate the countryside and this reached its peak during the Iron Age as the trees were cleared to make way for crops and livestock. Fire was used to clear the woodland and then grazing prevented the trees from regenerating. The climate, too, played a significant role. Because moorland is always wet the remains of plants do not rot, instead they accumulate and, as they compress, form a layer of peat over the soil. The minerals in the soil are washed away by high rainfall and those plants, such as heather and cotton grass, which prefer an infertile soil, flourish. After the Iron Age agriculture started to retreat from the moorland as the fertility became exhausted, though the remains of ancient settlements can still be seen on many moors today.

Grouse shooting was relatively unknown, apart from as a means to a meal, until the early nineteenth century and the uplands were primarily used as grazing for cattle, sheep, and deer. Ironically, given the clash of interests between the sheep farmers and the grouse moor managers today, it was this grazing that created the habitat that was suitable for grouse and their numbers grew. When standing in a grouse butt, it is hard to believe that the landscape that runs away all around you is largely a result of man's influence. These are some of the wildest parts of Britain, yet what we are trying to preserve today is largely our creation, albeit accidental. This is not to say that we should continue to let the uplands evolve without our influence; man has created the moorland to suit his own purposes and in doing so has created an area that is outstandingly beautiful with a diverse habitat benefiting a large range of flora and fauna. The evolution of the uplands, since the Iron Age, arose through economic interests and the fact that the main economic benefit today is from grouse shooting should be reason enough to continue the conservation of moorland for those interests.

SIMON GUDGEON

THE DECLINE OF MOORLAND

During the last hundred years the area of moorland managed for grouse shooting has fallen, during the same period the area of heather also suffered a reduction, which has led to a serious decline in the grouse population in some areas, especially Wales. The reduction in managed moorland and the reduction in heather are linked and this habitat loss will inevitably lead to a fall in the grouse population. The question now is, what is the cause and can it be reversed?

As stated in the previous section the evolution of the uplands was primarily driven by economics and the major contributor to the decline in heather moorland and grouse shooting is the same. After the First World War there was a massive demand for timber and after the Second World War the desire to be self-sufficient led to heavy subsidies being given for forestry, with large blocks of coniferous trees being planted. Since 1919 over 90% of the tree planting took place in Scotland where 10% of its total land area is now dominated by forest. Unlike the primeval woodlands that dominated the uplands before Neolithic Bronze Age man settled there, these forests do not sustain the diverse species that used to live

in the ancient Caledonian woodland. These original forests were home to large herbivores such as the aurochs and moose which kept clearings in the trees open allowing a mix of vegetation which would support other inhabitants such as grouse. During the first few years of a new forest, grouse will happily stay in the new habitat and flourish. The ground will often have been recently burnt or drained before planting so there will be plenty of young heather and planting will have disturbed the ground bringing grit to the surface. However, as the trees grow and block out the light, any heather remaining becomes rank and useless as a food source and soon the grouse, and most other species found on a grouse moor, die out.

Subsidies also led to an increase in sheep numbers which in turn caused a decline in heather moorland. Whilst sheep helped create the habitat that was suitable for grouse, overgrazing, by an excessive number of sheep, causes serious habitat loss. This is continuing today with subsidies being the sole reason that sheep are still on the hill. The problem with sheep and deer is that they are selective feeders, ie they select the food source that is most digestible, and if they are allowed to overgraze, then the less digestible vegetation, such as Molinia or Nardus, will become dominant. The design of their mouth also allows them to graze much closer than cattle and so they can do much more damage. Although grass is their preferred diet they will not eat the Molinia grass that dominates heather and forms the 'white ground' that heather cannot penetrate. When grass is in short supply they will eat heather, preferring the short new growth on the newly burnt areas. This can seriously slow the heather regeneration allowing other vegetation to become dominant and prevent the heather from becoming established. One sheep can destroy six acres of new heather growth in a year. Bilberry may also be grazed robbing grouse of a valuable winter food source. Most of this damage occurs in spring which can, in time, cause a food shortage for the grouse.

Modern techniques of shepherding exacerbate the problem. Whereas the shepherd used to move the flock around the moor ensuring no area became overgrazed, this no longer happens. Winter feeding tends to happen in the same place each day keeping an abnormally high number of sheep on a small area of ground which will eventually lead to heather loss. This winter 'fothering' usually takes place on the edge of the moor which also causes damage to other marginal species such as the black grouse. Better shepherding or wintering the sheep off the moor would help prevent this problem.

Landowners have to optimise the return on their land and that is one reason why grazing and grouse shooting operate on the same ground. Another is the fact that on many moors the ownership of the grazing rights and the shooting rights are owned by two different people. This can cause friction as the capital value of the land is almost entirely dependent on the average number of grouse shot over a ten year period, therefore heavy grazing on a grouse moor severely reduces the number of grouse it can sustain and the value of the land. To give an example, the shooting rights are worth around £3,000 per brace on a ten year average so if on a 2,000 acre moor the ten year average was 500 brace it would be worth £1,500,000. If, however, there were no grouse the grazing value of the land would be about £50 per acre making a total of £25,000. A considerable difference.

Another problem with sheep is that heavy grazing will lead to the spread of bracken. Bracken is a very invasive weed with no redeeming features; not only is it carcinogenic but it is also a safe haven for the tick which spreads louping ill. It is toxic to most grazing animals and once it has established itself, it eradicates all other plant species and is exceedingly difficult and expensive to get rid of. Some 16% of upland areas are covered by bracken and is increasing by 1-3% per annum. It spreads through overgrazing, burning heather too close to an area of bracken, and a rather vigorous root system. It also releases something called allelopthic compounds into the soil which inhibit the growth of other plant species. An altogether nasty piece of work and there are few ways of eradicating it. One way is to crush or cut the bracken until it is exhausted enabling other plant species to take hold but this is only possible on flattish ground. The most effective way is to spray the bracken by helicopter. This is very expensive and is rarely undertaken by anyone other than grouse moor managers and certainly never by sheep farmers.

Not only were the economic benefits of forestry and sheep, through subsidy, beginning to take their toll on the moorland, other economic factors also were also playing a role. The rise in labour costs led to a gradual decline in the number of gamekeepers, especially where louping ill was a problem. Good grouse keepers, in the correct number are, without doubt, the major influence on the success of a moor for grouse shooting. During the two World Wars, when many left the hill to fight overseas, predator numbers rose sharply putting severe pressure on the grouse. After the wars it was difficult to catch up with heather burning and predator control and many of the more marginal moors were lost to grouse shooting. Labour costs, too, were rising and many grouse managers tried to cut costs by reducing the number of keepers on the moor. This would start a

slow spiral of reduced bag numbers, lower income and yet more keepers losing their jobs, until the moor was no longer viable.

Although all moorland, whether managed for grouse shooting or not, has suffered from a loss of heather over the last hundred years, on those moors where grouse have been actively managed the heather loss has been much slower. The Game Conservancy Trust estimates that, in Scotland, nearly 1,000 square kilometres (247,000 acres) of heather would have been lost since 1945 were it not for grouse shooting.

Predator numbers are another factor which can make a moor no longer viable. The experiment at Langholm showed that large numbers of raptors can reduce the grouse population to a level where shooting can no longer take place and the management of the moor for grouse must cease. Unfortunately, because Langholm also suffered a severe loss of heather during the period of the experiment, it was not possible to conclusively prove that the decline was due solely to predation. However, I shall save the thorny problem of raptors for the chapter on predators, suffice to say that unless the RSPB and the Government exercises a little common sense soon, the loss of heather and habitat in the uplands is going to be catastrophic.

THE HEATHER BEETLE

A small and very tenacious beetle can also contribute to the decline of heather moorland. The effect of the heather beetle can often be seen when walking on the moor in August. The foxy-red discolouration of great swathes of heather providing evidence of its presence. Although this does not normally lead to the permanent loss of heather it can, if the soil conditions support the vigorous Molinia grass, lead to that species replacing heather on affected areas. It also seriously affects the carrying capacity of the moor as the damage it causes results in the depletion of the food available to the grouse during the winter months. If this occurs it is essential to lower the number of sheep to reduce competition for what healthy heather there is left.

The heather beetle is tiny and very difficult to find. They hibernate during winter in heather litter, moss, or up to two inches deep in the soil, which makes their eradication during heather burning extremely difficult as all but the hottest fire will leave them unscathed underground. In spring the young beetle emerges and starts to feed on the heather. The female will lay up to 700 eggs in sphagnum moss from April until the end of June. Because they are so small, when airborne they are very much at the mercy of the winds which is why evidence of damage is often seen in long strips as the beetles are carried off by the prevailing wind. The eggs hatch within four weeks and the young larvae climb up the heather to feed, once fully grown they drop back onto the ground and burrow down to pupate and emerge as immature adults towards the end of August.

From a grouse manager's point of view there is nothing that can be done to eradicate this pest. Burning is ineffective and there is no selective insecticide to control it. The best thing to do is continue with conventional burning practices as most of the heather will recover naturally from the effects of the beetle. However, there are several of things which can help to control this pest. The first and most effective of which is a small parasitic wasp - asecodes (Entodon) mento - that lays its eggs on the beetle larvae which hatches and then feeds on its host. Weather, too, can control the outbreak of the beetle. Although they are largely resilient to frosts and cold winters, tucked up as they are under the heather litter, cool dry springs, however, do not provide the humidity that the eggs need in order to hatch. If these weather conditions occur, and larvae

numbers are small, nearly every one of them will be preyed upon by the wasp causing a crash in numbers that will take several years to recover. Thirdly, the ladybird - predator of greenfly and gardener's friend - will turn its attention to the larvae as will a parasitic fungi, Beauveria bassiana.

THE RESTORATION
OF HEATHER MOORLAND

The alarm bells should have rung when the letter introducing the moor began with the phrase "I think you should look at this with your optimistic hat on". A sentence that would have repelled lesser souls and had all but the most enthusiastic optimist running in the other direction. Not so Martin Vallance. Ignoring most who advised against it, he bought the shooting rights to Arkleside, in the Yorkshire Dales, and set about restoring this 2,000 acre moor to its former glory. Possibly, given his dedication and enthusiasm, even exceeding it.

Arkleside had suffered badly from overgrazing and grouse numbers had been declining steadily over the years. Indeed parts of it were described by one consultant as 'a large area of moor....otherwise horribly overgrazed and largely useless for grouse.' Another agent concluded that less than 15-20% of the whole moor was actually suitable for grouse. The moor was in serious decline and had Martin not come along when he did, Arkleside would probably have ceased to be a grouse moor by now. The Common Agricultural Policy, the bane of many a moor owner's life, encourages farmers to overstock the hill as a subsidy is received

for each animal. This has lead to the current dramatic fall in lamb prices and severe damage to heather, a point perfectly illustrated at the boundary fence at Arkleside. On the Arkleside side of the fence the ground is 'white ground' and covered in grasses and sedges. Over the boundary, where sheep numbers are kept low, it is a carpet of purple heather. Overgrazing has been the main cause in heather loss this century and if it had not been reduced Arkleside would not have recovered.

This moor is a good example with which to illustrate the many techniques used for moorland restoration as the problems tackled here are the same as on many moors. Restoring moorland is a relatively simple exercise, the main aim being to replace the grass area or 'white ground' with suitable habitat for grouse. This will primarily be heather with a mix of other vegetation, such as cotton grass, and bilberry. Restoration is, however, both time consuming and costly as it takes several years before any results become evident. During that time all the ancillary costs associated with grouse moor management, such as gamekeepers and vehicles, have to be met. Thus, as well as deep pockets, it takes a great deal of dedication and commitment to achieve results. It is a measure of this commitment that, rather than spending the same amount of money buying let days, people such as Martin Vallance are prepared to devote their time and money for a smaller return, and in some years no return at all.

Arkleside consists of a patchwork of several different moors with differing, and sometimes conflicting, ownership and rights which prevents Martin from having complete control over the whole area. Whilst he was able to buy the shooting rights over the whole area, he does not have control over the grazing. He has the shooting rights to two 450 acre blocks known as Arkleside and Hindlethwaite, and the freehold and shooting rights, but no grazing rights, to West Scrafton, which is about 1,000 acres. However he does have absolute control over High Pasture having bought the freehold and grazing rights of this small (150 acres), but important, piece of moor.

Much of the moorland had stunted heather growing amongst the grass and if the grazing pressure could be reduced this would allow the heather to once again flourish. By working with the farmers, Martin was able to convince them to enter Arkleside and Hindlethwaite into the Countryside Stewardship Scheme (CSS) which encourages greater environmental care through subsidy. Essentially the farmer gets an area payment for good management rather than a payment per head of sheep. This has led to over 1,000 sheep being taken off the hill and already the benefits are being seen as heather is beginning to push its way through the grass and will, in time, become the dominant species. By carefully burning the moor and keeping the sheep off in winter, the habitat for grouse will gradually improve and their numbers will rise. It is fortunate that the neighbouring moors are well kept and have a good stock of grouse as this has helped the moor survive over the years. When Martin took over the moor the few grouse there were in marginal territories on, or close to, the boundaries. They are now beginning to re-establish territories further into the moor as the habitat becomes more suitable.

The largest block of moorland at Arkleside is West Scrafton where he purchased the freehold and shooting rights. Unfortunately the moor is subject to a rather quirky system of grazing rights which are superior to the freehold and sporting rights. The moor has what are called 'gaits' and each gait gives the holder the right to graze one sheep on the moor. Eight gaits gives the right to graze a horse. West Scrafton is subject to 889 gaits which are split between four different farmers and so trying to get agreement to reduce grazing pressure has been difficult. "This is the most difficult area because there has to be agreement between four different

SIMON GUDGEON

farmers and myself, all of whom having legitimate claims to a livelihood on the land," says Martin. "I am well aware that any scheme that I put forward must be of positive benefit to these farmers - I would like to see less sheep, but their level of income must be maintained or improved in such a situation." It is this spirit of conciliation that is reaping benefits, for it is the gaitholder who has the stronger hand when it comes to moorland management and it is important that the two interests work together for the benefit of each other. Most farmers agree that moorland which is good for grouse is also good for sheep. They know that grouse are not the sheep's enemy - their problem is other sheep, for an excessive number of sheep will reduce the food supply for them all. This is reflected in Martin's Arkleside motto: *pessimus inimicus ovis alius ovis est* - the worst enemy of a sheep is another sheep.

Indeed, grouse moors do benefit from some grazing as this improves the bulk or 'biomass' of the heather. What is important is getting the right balance. The main damage from sheep occurs in two areas; firstly from winter grazing when the sheep will eat heather in preference to grass. This directly competes with the grouse whose sole food source in winter is heather and the stock of good heather in winter will determine the carrying capacity of the moor. Secondly, the sheep will graze on the new heather shoots growing on freshly burnt areas. Because they have no teeth on their bottom jaw they pull the young heather out by its roots rather than biting it off and a single sheep can destroy six acres of young heather in a year. This will allow the grasses to become dominant and the result, unless grazing pressure is reduced, will be white ground, with Molinia or other grasses dominating.

On West Scrafton there is a good chance that the existing heather will be able to regenerate if the grazing pressure is reduced. Agreement has now been reached to put it into the Countryside Stewardship Scheme which will halve the number of sheep on the moor in winter.

High Pasture, on the other hand, presents a different set of problems. This 150 acre moor has been entered into the CSS and is now completely enclosed by fences to exclude the sheep, however there is insufficient existing heather amongst the dominant grass species for regeneration to take place and so a different approach was necessary to restore this area. In the world of moorland restoration there are two names which ought to be carved in stone and revered by all those who shoot grouse. Richard May and Geoff Eyre have achieved staggering results through determination and enthusiasm prompted by their passion for grouse shooting and their commitment to the conservation of other moorland birds. Neither are scientifically trained yet have achieved the alchemy of moorland management; turning white ground back into heather moorland.

There are two ways to tackle this problem, the first of which is regeneration from existing seed. Heather seed is remarkably resilient and will lie dormant in the ground for many years before germinating. This is why heather will start to grow again in areas where forestry has been cleared. Peat samples are taken from the moor at a depth of 50mm and 100mm and the samples are then treated in laboratory conditions to see if there is any heather seed which will germinate. If it does then the ground has a good seed bank which should grow if the grass is sprayed off and then, after using a pasture topper to smash the tussocks, the area is scarified to clear away the dead grass and bring the peat to the surface. This brings the dormant seeds to the top where they are exposed to light, heat and frost which will help stimulate germination. This is quite a slow process and the grass has to be continually checked whilst the young heather plants take hold.

The other method of regeneration has only recently been developed and refined and involves re-sowing the ground with fresh seed. If there is insufficient existing heather to regenerate then removing sheep from areas of moorland will not lead to a resurgence of heather. This was the problem faced by Richard May at Macclesfield, where he has a 200 acre moor, and by Geoff Eyre, in the Peak District, who has managed a moor for many years. Both had large areas of species poor Molinia grassland which they have transformed into moorland with a much greater diversity of both plants and animals than was there before. This has been achieved through hard work, experimentation, and investment.

When tackling areas of savannah-like grassland the first stage is to spray off the grass with a herbicide, once the grass has died off it will be burnt. If it is a dry moor a pasture topper is then used to break up the tussocks prior to reseeding. Geoff Eyre has pioneered the work on reseeding and developed machinery to collect the seeds and sow them. Heather seeds are collected in late autumn or early winter after the first few frosts have turned them brown in the flower pod. They will then be laid out on trays and dried using big fans, and if the outside air is frosty so much the better. The seeds can either be left in the pod or separated and graded, depending on how they are going to be sown. Heather seeds are so tiny that if one kilo of heather seed were to be sown at the same rate as maize it would be sufficient to cover 1,000 acres.

The seeds can be treated in different ways which will give different germination rates. The first of these is to sow the seeds neat in the pod which will mean germination is slower. The next method is to smoke them. It used to be thought that it was the heat of the fire, during heather burning, that stimulated germination of the heather seed. However, modern science has discovered that it is, in fact, a chemical in the smoke which is responsible. Thus by subjecting the seeds to the smoke of burning heather they will begin to germinate. Science has also isolated the chemical in the smoke that the seeds react to and if they are soaked in a solution containing this chemical the germination rate can increase from 5% to 78%.

There is a further treatment that the seeds can be subjected to if one is prepared to take the risk that the growing conditions are going to be just right after sowing, i.e. warm and damp. This method is called chitting and involves slowly warming the seeds, in a damp condition, until they just begin to split prior to sending out their first shoot. The seeds are then sown immediately and, providing there is no dry weather for the first two weeks they will establish themselves at an incredible rate with a much higher success rate than would otherwise be achieved. Unfortunately, if a period of dry weather occurs within the first few weeks, when using this method, all will be lost.

If the seeds are kept in the pods they can be broadcast from an ordinary fertilizer spreader on the back of a tractor. If, however the ground is unsuitable for tractors the seeds that have been removed from the pods are so fine they can be mixed with water and sprayed onto the ground by helicopter. At High Pasture, on Arkleside, both methods were employed to sow pods that had been untreated and seeds that had been smoked and also soaked in a chemical solution. A third of the moor had been sprayed and burnt prior to reseeding in July. By October of the same year, the seedlings were beginning to appear, small green shoots heralding the return of heather to this part of the moor. The small shoots will be killed off by the first winter frosts but the root system will survive and in spring the shoots will once again push through the peat. On dry ground the first shoots will appear in small hollows left by tractor tyres or footprints as these areas are slightly damper than their surroundings. On wet moors, however, it is advisable to leave the tussocks of the dead grasses as they are above the waterlogged area and will create nursery beds for the heather seeds to germinate. The successful germination of the heather seeds on High Pasture will create areas of heather that can gradually spread into the other ground. It is only a matter of time before the grouse once more colonise this moor as they move in from the well stocked neighbouring moors.

Richard May's problem, however, is no longer a lack of heather, but a lack of grouse. When he first started his regeneration project in 1991, the 200 acre moor was like a savannah with nothing but grass. One has to admire the optimism of someone who sets out to create a grouse moor where there is no heather and not one single grouse. Such a Herculean task takes an enormous amount of enthusiasm and dedication. It also takes a very understanding wife! With grant aid he restored and rebuilt the dry stone wall around the moor to prevent further grazing and, following the techniques mentioned above, now has a moor that has a good stock of heather which will soon be ready for rotational burning. The moor is becoming a haven for other moorland birds such as the curlew. The first two pairs of which nested in 2000 and on the lower parts of the moor over 50 snipe were seen on an area where sphagnum moss is regenerating in the bog flushes. As well as snipe and curlew, meadow pipits and skylarks are all there in numbers and this year a covey of wild grey partridge were seen on the moor. Hares, too, are increasing as the control of vermin and the improved habitat encourage them to colonise the moor. Unfortunately there are no well managed neighbouring moors nearby and consequently no grouse to move into the ideal habitat that has been created. He is relying on the generosity of other moor owners to let him catch up a few grouse and release them. We walked the moor a few weeks after he had released the first half dozen hoping to catch a glimpse of them or at least hear them - sadly we didn't, although trying to find six grouse on 200 acres brought the words 'needle' and 'haystack' to mind. He is going to release some more birds in the near future and I hope that his efforts will be rewarded when he hears his first grouse on the moor. Standing in the middle of this moor, surveying all the work that had gone into this project and all the time and money invested, which, even when finished, is barely going to provide half a day's shooting, it becomes obvious that shooting grouse is not his main motivating factor; it is the creation and conservation of a habitat that he loves.

Improving the habitat for other moorland species is high on Martin Vallance's list of priorities too, not only on the higher ground where the red grouse live but also lower down. He is planting new woodland along the gills that run up to the moor to create habitat for black grouse and, by controlling predators, should be able to encourage wild grey partridge onto the low ground. By improving the wetland and bog flushes the numbers of snipe, curlew, and other waders will increase, whilst the dwarf shrub heathland will see the return of skylarks and merlins. The rewards for regenerating a piece of countryside such as this are never financial, but the satisfaction of knowing that you have left something in a better state than you found it and the enjoyment of shooting your own moor with friends

MOORLAND GRAZING: HIGHLAND CATTLE V SHEEP

They have short legs, are rather hairy, and have a pleasant disposition. The main subject in many a Victorian artist's depiction of a halcyon moorland scene may also be the grouse moor manager's answer to overgrazing and the upland farmer's answer to low sheep prices. Highland cattle numbers have been in decline ever since sheep became the universal panacea for mass meat production. Interestingly their decline has closely shadowed that of the grouse.

Highland cattle are one of Britain's oldest breeds and still flourish in areas where meagre grazing and harsh weather would prevent other breeds from surviving. They are, however, becoming increasingly popular on grouse moors where recent research by the World Pheasant Association (WPA) in conjunction with The Game Conservancy Trust has highlighted the advantages of Highland cattle over other grazers in terms of grouse moor management. Their most enthusiastic ambassador is Keith Howman, President of the WPA, who keeps a small fold (the collective noun for Highlanders, never refer to them as a herd in his presence) of Highland cattle on his son's grouse moor in the Scottish Highlands where all black-faced sheep have been banished. He firmly believes that these hardy cattle are more beneficial to grouse moors than any other species as their method of grazing actually improves the habitat for the grouse.

It is certainly true that some grazing is necessary to keep moorland grouse-friendly. Research has shown that where less than 10% of the heather biomass, or bulk, is grazed, grouse numbers are low, and they start to decline if over 20% is grazed. Highland cattle at the right density of about one per 10 hectares eat about 15% of the biomass which is perfect for grouse, and compares very favourably with sheep.

It is not only the amount they graze but also how they graze that benefits a grouse moor. Sheep are nibblers and can destroy new heather growth on burnt areas allowing grass to take hold. The mouth of the Highland cow is larger and cannot bite the young heather so allowing the burnt areas to regenerate unhindered. Unlike sheep, they are non-selective grazers which means that they have the ability to graze all species, rather than selecting those with the greatest digestibility so they will tackle the insidious Molinia grass that dominates poor white ground where grouse will not flourish.

Feeding areas for Highland cattle can be strategically placed to help with heather management. Feeders placed in areas of bracken will allow their large hooves to break down and trample bracken until young heather can become re-established. Also, by feeding Highland cattle on areas of tall rank heather, near woodland where it cannot be burnt, their large hooves will break down the vegetation allowing light to penetrate and young heather to regenerate.

Perhaps one of the greatest advantages of having Highland cattle on the moor, from the grouse's point of view, is the vast quantities of dung they produce. This is very attractive to insects, much more so than sheep droppings, and up to a thousand can inhabit one pat. In a single year a cow will create an estimated 200lb of insect life. These high protein invertebrates are a necessary part of grouse chicks' diet for the first few weeks of their life and if there is not a plentiful supply they will not survive. The movement of the fold during the day and the distribution of the cattle within the fold ensures that the dung is widely spread over the moor. The WPA/GCT research, using GPS, recorded that the cattle moved about 630 metres per day. A slightly less scientific approach was taken when the effect of midges on cattle was being looked at. The scientist carrying out the research noticed that during warm weather, when the midge density was high, the cattle move up to higher ground where there was a breeze which kept the midges down. In order to assess the midge density he rolled up his sleeve and counted the number of bites in a given period. As someone whose loathing of midges is not reciprocated by them I have a great admiration for anyone taking this approach in the furtherance of knowledge.

Highland cattle do seem to have advantages over sheep on a grouse moor, although problems with the latter only arise if there are too many of them and if they are kept on the hill over winter. I remember the comment of one gamekeeper, standing on a fellside overlooking an area of white ground with a large flock of sheep. 'Look at it,' he said with despair, 'it's polluted with woolly maggots.' This is not a new discovery, the Rev. Mr Singer, Minister of Kirkpatrick, wrote, in a discourse on sheep husbandry, in 1803 that "the evils complained of have arisen from an extreme in that system, rather than from the nature of the stock introduced." He proposed a mixed system of cattle and sheep as the former "consume the rank grasses and render the pasture more wholesome." He concluded that "cattle alone, are not a safe stock; sheep reared exclusively, turn all into waste."

There is still much work to be done in assessing the impact of Highland cattle on grouse moors but, quite apart from the aesthetic pleasure to be gained from watching these gentle creatures munch their way through the vegetation, they do appear to have a role to play in grouse moor management and are a pleasant antidote to the ubiquitous sheep.

MOORLAND FLORA

A grouse moor supports a rich diversity of plants and mosses. A few species, such as purple moor-grass (Molinia caerulea) and mat grass (Nardus stricta), are detrimental to the moor. They have no nutritional value and are invasive, tending to dominate the sward, creating large areas of white ground that are of little benefit to any of the species that live on the moor. There are myriad varieties of mosses and grasses that contribute to the rich ecosystem on the moor; the mosses that grow around the bog flushes are host to a legion of insects thus providing food for young grouse and curlew. The highly nutritious cotton grass buds in early spring build up the strength of the hen grouse before she starts laying and brooding, while the wavy hair grass colonises the freshly burnt areas and prevents erosion whilst the heather re-establishes itself. Having deer grass and sheep's fescue on the moor helps to sustain a multiple land use as the sheep and deer will prefer to eat these species, in summer, rather than heather.

Then there are the plants that feature in the grouse diet. The main one is certainly heather ling which will provide most of the nutritional needs of grouse throughout the winter. In summer the percentage of heather in the diet will fall to around 50% as other plants are eaten. The most important of these is the bilberry of which grouse will eat the stem, buds, flowers and berries. Other plant varieties that contribute to the grouse diet are illustrated on these pages.

The presence of this huge diversity sustains the moor and its inhabitants and is one reason why a good grouse moor will have only a 60 % heather covering with the balance made up of these other beneficial plant varieties.

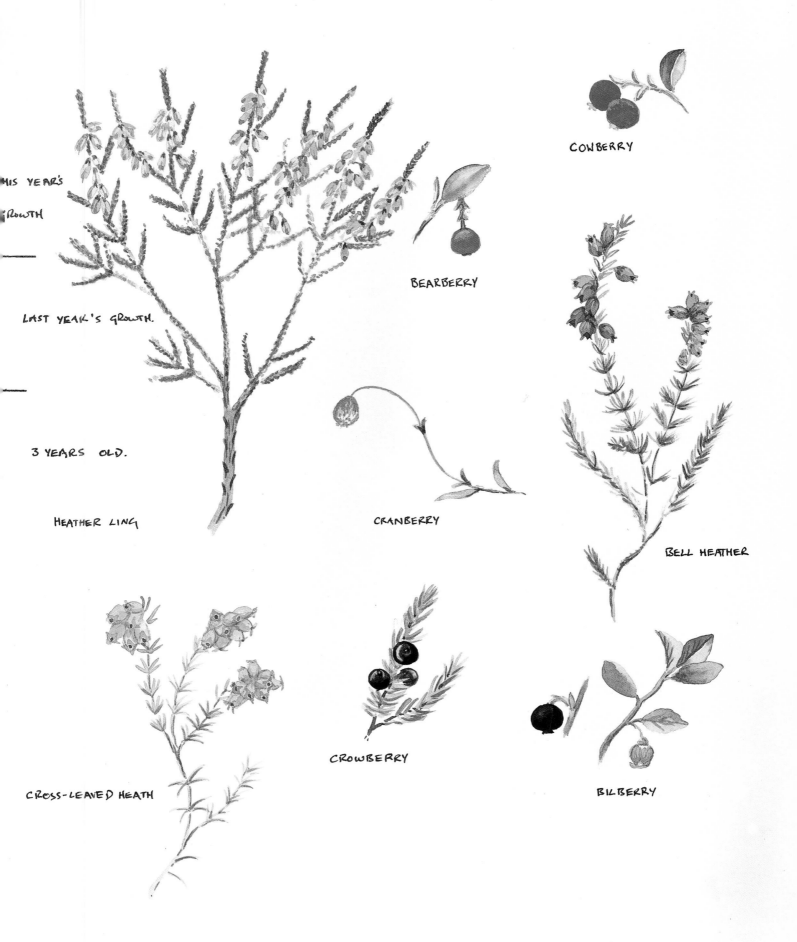

THIS YEAR'S GROWTH

LAST YEAR'S GROWTH.

3 YEARS OLD.

HEATHER LING

BEARBERRY

COWBERRY

CRANBERRY

BELL HEATHER

CROSS-LEAVED HEATH

CROWBERRY

BILBERRY

GAMEKEEPING

INTRODUCTION

Gamekeeping is, without doubt, the single most important aspect of grouse moor management and a good grouse keeper is beyond price. We are not so much talking about a job as a way of life. A passion, with an exceptional level of dedication. I spent several days with a keeper in Yorkshire, whilst doing the research for this book, and only then did I realise the depth of feeling that they have for the birds under their care. Every morning, before dawn he would be onto the moor to watch and listen whilst the moor came alive. The grouse calling to each other before the sky had begun to lighten from the east would tell him if there was anything there that wanted to breakfast on one of his precious birds. Every evening just before dusk he would do the same whilst the moor went to sleep. It was a rare treat to be able to be on the moor at that time and experience those sounds, but it was a bitterly cold February and I have nothing but admiration for someone who does it every day. In winter the days are short and the conditions often harsh. In summer, with the longer days, this can mean that he will be on the moor at 3.30am for the dawn and 11.00pm for dusk.

In grouse moor management there are several factors that will determine grouse numbers and the success of a moor. The major ones are spring breeding weather, disease, habitat and predator control. No-one has control of the former and whilst the effects of disease can be lessened it cannot be prevented. However, with careful habitat preservation and effective predator control the negative effects of the first two can be lessened ensuring that in a bad year the crash is not too severe and in a good year there is a boom. It is the keeper who carries out these duties and will, if effective, dramatically improve grouse stocks.

For keepering to be effective you have to have the right sort of person. Someone who is highly effective at predator control but also, and more importantly, someone who has a feeling or an empathy with grouse. He will understand their ways and their behaviour. In addition, there must be the right number of keepers. One for every 3,000 acres is the ideal, whose sole responsibility is the wellbeing of the grouse. The gamekeeper who has to look

after the low ground shoot, stalking and fishing as well as doing a bit of grouse keepering, will not produce many grouse. On the other hand, those moors where the numbers of keepers has risen in recent years, have shown a dramatic increase in grouse numbers. To illustrate this point there is a small moor in Aberdeenshire which had not been shot for four seasons. A change in the keepering team resulted in a 100 brace day after only two seasons, the first time this had been achieved for 20 years. Since then an all-time record has been broken with a 156 brace day. On another moor in Northumberland a new tenant took over nearly ten years ago. At the time he was told that the moor would never see a 100 brace day again. There was only one full time and one part time keeper to cover nearly 20,000 acres. Now there are five full time keepers, and in 1997 the moor produced 5,000 brace in 50 days of shooting - an average of 100 brace per day.

Gamekeepers not only manage one of the few truly wild gamebirds but also act as guardians of the rich diversity of the heather moorlands. Through predator control and maintenance of habitat they provide the ideal conditions in which many moorland species can flourish. In a recent survey conducted by the RSPB and The Game Conservancy Trust it was found that species such as golden plovers and lapwings were five times as abundant on grouse moors compared with other moors, and curlews twice as common. If any justification for grouse shooting were needed on wildlife conservation grounds this is it.

The gamekeeper's year is a long one and there is no lull after the shooting season. As well as the year round task of predator control and the seasonal heather burning, the keeper has to find time to repair or make new butts, do the grouse counts, control bracken and grass, gritting, worm counts, direct dosing and much, much more.

PREDATOR CONTROL

The grouse's enemies are many and if there are to be enough birds for the shooting season they must be controlled. Many of the worst offenders are protected and therefore do not come into this chapter. They are the birds of prey whose increasing numbers do not bode well for the future of the delicate balance in the uplands. They will be dealt with in the section on predators. Here I will concentrate on those predators which, though they regard the grouse as a tasty morsel, can be controlled.

Whilst trying to cover this subject reasonably comprehensively I am conscious of the fact that the vast majority of gamekeepers who read this will know far more than I and so it would be pointless trying to make this into an instruction manual on predator control. Similarly, those who know very little about predator control and have no need, apart from general interest, in learning more, would probably find a technical explanation of how to set a snare rather tedious. So please forgive me if, at times, my coverage is rather brief or at others not brief enough. For a more detailed description of predator control see Red Grouse and Moorland Management, an excellent booklet published by The Game Conservancy Trust.

Moorland predator control falls into three main areas all requiring a different approach. Firstly the fox, secondly stoats and weasels, and lastly crows and magpies. On moors close to the coast herring gulls and black-backed gulls can cause problems when grouse chicks are hatching but these can be legally controlled and shooting them is the most efficient method.

FOXES

The sheer numbers of foxes that are culled each year shows why all the ground nesting birds on moors do so well. At Langholm, before grouse shooting ended due to excessive predation by hen harriers and peregrine falcons, they averaged 200 foxes a year. This is probably why a ground nesting bird such as the hen harrier was able to increase from 2 nests to 21 in five years. The devastation this number of foxes could do if unchecked is colossal and the effort to cull this number in order to protect grouse is enormous. The fact that such large numbers can be culled year on

SIMON GUDGEON

year is indicative of a rising population. In many parts of the uplands the fox was extinct at the turn of the century but has established a hold as the number of gamekeepers has dwindled and managed grouse moors have declined.

Foxes are far more abundant than nature intended because their natural enemies, such as the wolf and lynx, are extinct. They need, therefore, to be controlled throughout the year and it helps if neighbouring areas follow the same policy. Pity the keeper with low ground on his boundaries where foxes can roam without let or hindrance for he has a Herculean task in trying to protect his grouse. This is especially true of moors with adjacent forestry blocks. The most damage is done during breeding time when hens on their nests and whole broods of chicks will be taken but grouse remain at risk all year round.

The methods of fox control are many and varied from lamping, to snaring and lurchers. Lamping at night using a high powered lamp and a rifle is particularly effective if the ground is relatively easily covered by a four wheel drive or ATV. Once spotted they can be called in by squeaking, a method that is devastatingly effective if done by an expert (my attempts have always sent the fox in the other direction and reduced the keeper into fits of giggles).

Snaring is more skilful and requires a degree of understanding of fox behaviour. It is particularly effective on low ground surrounding the moor where the snares can be set in woodland and along fence lines thus catching the fox before it has set foot on the moor. Foxes do not like jumping fences or any other barrier and will walk along such an impediment seeking a way through rather than over. So it is always worth looking for gaps in fencing when trying to spot fox runs. These are ideal places to set a snare. I met one gamekeeper who would create a barrier, using branches, along the entire width of a wood. He would leave a gap every so often and set a snare in the gap. Any fox crossing the wood would come across the barrier, find the gap, and be caught in the snare.

Whilst snares have to be checked every twenty-four hours human scent on or near can negate their effectiveness. Most keepers will avoid washing their hands with soap if they are handling their snares and traps and are careful not to get creosote on their hands when climbing fences. Gun oil, too, can be a problem so laying a gun on the ground should be avoided when checking snares. Also when checking snares keepers will walk along the fox run and step over the snare, continuing along the run so that their scent does not stop abruptly and make the fox suspicious.

Middens, or as they are less pleasantly known, stink pits, are small areas where smelly bait is buried to attract foxes. Dead sheep or other carrion are normally used although one of the most effective baits is another fox's carcass. This seems to attract foxes by arousing their curiosity and maybe their territorial instincts. Various paths are cut with a strimmer, leading to the midden and then snares are placed on the paths inside the midden. Four or five middens with 20-30 snares are much easier to check daily than the same number of snares spread over a large area of low ground and will be just as effective.

Fox control is a high priority in spring when one of the most effective methods of control is to bolt foxes from their dens using terriers. The fresh diggings of the vixen as she prepares the den are relatively easy to spot, although too close an inspection may leave scent around the den which will panic the fox into abandoning it. Once all the exits have been found those that cannot be watched by a man with a shotgun should be covered with a purse net. Another alternative is to have a lurcher standing by to catch any unseen foxes. Lurchers for foxes do not need to be fast but they do have to be tenacious and aggressive. A greyhound crossed with a bull terrier, doberman, or German shepherd is ideal as it will kill a fox quickly and cleanly. Once all the exits are covered then a terrier is introduced into the den. The role of the terrier is to locate the fox and then come out of the den allowing the fox to bolt so it can be shot or caught in the purse net.

Finally, one of the most physically demanding methods of locating foxes is tracking them in freshly fallen snow. Whilst the tracks are relatively easy to follow a fox can travel up to 30 miles in a night and so following those tracks the next day can be a rather strenuous activity. The fox will often double back on itself and use other tricks to mislead any pursuer. Having a good lurcher present is a help as the fox can often catch you unawares and be out of range before a shot can be taken.

CROWS

The crow family provides a number of predators of grouse but by far the most significant are the carrion crow and hooded crow. Magpies, jackdaws, and rooks can have an effect, especially on lower moors, but methods used to control crows will also apply to them. It is in spring and summer when all the damage is done with crows eating both the eggs and chicks of all ground nesting birds. This is also the time when the most effective method of control, trapping, takes place. Crows are territorial birds during the breeding season and it is these birds that do all the damage. Their territorial behaviour makes trapping them all the

easier. A side entrance Larsen trap, with a captive bird to entice the territorial crow into the trap, is highly effective in spring. These birds try to chase the intruder away and as they walk around the trap they will find the opening and get caught. Finding a live decoy can be a problem although many keepers keep a couple of birds alive through the winter to use in spring. Alternatively making a nest with a few eggs can entice a bird into the trap which can then be used as a live decoy.

Cage traps are semi-permanent structures that operate on a similar principle in spring, but in summer they can be baited to attract non-territorial birds into them. Siting them well away from paths is necessary to stop misguided ramblers from releasing the decoy to wreak havoc on the local bird population. The road to hell is paved with good intentions.

STOATS, MINK AND POLECATS.

The most important predators that can be legally controlled are certainly foxes and crows as they will have the greatest impact on grouse numbers. The effect of stoats, mink, ferrets, and perhaps even weasels on grouse numbers will depend on habitat and the abundance of alternative prey species such as rabbits. Prior to myxomatosis stoats were far more prevalent and so by controlling rabbits it may be possible to reduce stoat numbers, although they will adapt to a diet of grouse if plentiful. Mink, too, will eat rabbits and will often leave their natural habitat near water if alternative food is abundant. All these species are part of the marten genus known as mustelids and will take grouse, eggs and chicks and should be controlled.

Stoats are normally the most prevalent of this group and will kill grouse, usually the incubating hen, with a bite to the jugular. They are also notorious for removing the eggs from nests, rolling them to a safe haven where they will suck out the contents. These safe havens are usually in the stoat's favourite hiding place, old stone walls, where large collections of sucked eggs, sometimes in excess of a hundred, can be found.

They can be controlled in two ways, firstly, as already mentioned by reducing their alternative food sources. Secondly by the more direct method of shooting and trapping. Mink and polecats, which are usually just escaped ferrets, should be totally eradicated from the moor with an intensive offensive against the stoat in spring and early summer. Because traps have to be checked every 24 hours it is not always practical to run trap lines for mustelids all year round, especially as some trap lines will have over a hundred traps in them, spread over a large area.

The best method of trapping them is using spring traps, usually Fenn traps, in a tunnel with a little bait such as rabbit liver smeared on the plate. If a female is caught in season then a little of her urine squeezed onto the plate of the trap will prove irresistible to any male in the vicinity. The tunnels will be placed next to walls, hedges, banks or piles of stones, although they are also very effective if placed out in the moor in tunnels. They should also be placed around crow traps to catch anything that is attracted to the carrion therein. A particularly effective site is to place a pole across a stream with a two foot length of wire netting in the middle forming a tunnel. The spring trap can then be placed in the tunnel and catch anything crossing the stream. As with snares there is a problem with scent and so any trap should be weathered before it is used to get rid of the smell of grease and human scent. Lubrication of the trap should be done with a natural oil, such as fish oil, or beeswax.

HEATHER BURNING

Heather burning is one of the most important aspects of grouse moor management, although the benefits to grouse were discovered by accident. In the first half of the nineteenth century, before grouse shooting had become accessible or popular, shoot rents were low and the majority of the income generated from moorland was from grazing rents for sheep. In order to maintain sufficient food supply for their flock shepherds had to burn the heather to provide young growth for feeding. The object, as set out in the lease, was to burn one-tenth of the moor per annum and the shepherds or farmers tended to choose the windiest day and burn huge blocks of moor. Although their methods were unsophisticated, and their intentions were solely for the benefit of the sheep, judging from the few bags recorded at this time it would seem that the grouse benefitted and stocks were plentiful.

Between 1850 and 1873 grouse shooting became more popular. The advent of the railways improved accessibility, it was the heyday of London gunmaking, each firm vying to have the latest and best design, and there was a general increase in wealth.

All this combined with the fact that grouse shooting was becoming fashionable meant that shoot rents were rapidly approaching, and then overtaking, grazing rents. An example of this was at Faskally where two moors offered for rent in 1830 for £8 were let for £800 by 1880. This combined with the decline of the sheep market as Australia's wool production started to rise, meant that the economic value of grouse shooting was now firmly established. Indeed, if grouse shooting had not become so financially lucrative for the landowner most of our heather moorland would, by today, have been lost to agriculture and forestry as has happened all over Europe.

This meant that the moors were now being managed for grouse production rather than sheep and the shooting tenant took over the responsibility for burning the heather. One would have thought that now the moor was being burnt for the benefit of the grouse an increase in the yield would result, this sadly was not to be the case. The majority of shooting at this time was over dogs and long heather was the ideal. The term 'keeper's delight' was applied to heather over three foot high as it provided better cover for shooting over dogs thus making the birds more approachable and so easier to shoot. Thus less and less burning was undertaken. In many instances the reduction was from one-tenth of the moor to one-hundredth, and as a consequence grouse numbers started to fall. This came to peak in 1872 and 1873 which were years of exceptionally high disease and grouse numbers crashed.

However, not all moors had stopped burning. As a consequence of the reduction in burning there was not enough young heather and grass for the sheep and some farmers had leased the sporting rights along with the grazing rights so that they could continue to burn. On these areas the grouse continued to flourish and it became accepted that burning was necessary to manage the moor for grouse. Indeed, in 1871 and 1873 the Game Laws Commission, whilst investigating the relations of sporting and farming interests, found that the heather conditions for sheep and grouse were similar. Thus a more intelligent method of moorland management was adopted whereby the farming and sporting interests worked together to provide habitat that would sustain both sheep and grouse.

The objects of burning are to provide a mixed habitat for grouse containing patches of different aged heather. Older heather at the edges of the burnt ground provides areas for nesting and concealment, although grouse have been known to nest on open burnt ground. The edges of burnt ground also provide a reference point for territorial cocks. The burnt areas are used by the grouse for sunning and dusting, sometimes they even fly in through the smoke and dust themselves in the warm ash. They also use the recently burnt areas to roost which can help to reduce disease. Younger heather provides food for the grouse, the nutritional content of young heather being superior having more nitrogen, phosphorus and potassium. The patchwork of burnt ground will also attract sheep away from the fringes of heather moorland where overgrazing can occur.

In addition, burning can provide fire breaks and reduce the risk of large scale fires such as occurred in Yorkshire in the last century. These fires occur during very dry weather and often lead to the peat being burned away to a depth of several feet. I visited one moor where huge boulders were visible, some five or six feet high, which had been exposed by those fires as the peat was gradually burnt away. A fire of this intensity would destroy not only the roots of the heather but also much of the heather seed. However even after a fire such as this the heather can recover and the fact that the moor today has a very good covering of heather is a testament to careful management. It also means that the depth of peat is very shallow, only a few inches in places, and thus fairly dry, making it less likely to suffer large doses of strongyle worm.

Burning will help clean up diseased areas of the moor by destroying the strongyle worm eggs and larvae, and the ticks that cause louping ill. In 1906 the Committee of Inquiry on grouse disease, headed by Lord Lovat, which resulted in the excellent book 'The Grouse in Health and in Disease' (still obtainable from specialist second hand book dealers), concluded that the "patch or strip method of burning must as far as possible be pursued in order to segregate the birds, and thereby lessen the risk of infection by the strongyle worm and the coccidium." If there are large numbers of patches providing plenty of nutritional young heather, the grouse are less likely to congregate in one area to feed and consequently spread disease.

The Game Conservancy Trust's recommendations are that mature heather is burnt in strips 20-30 metres wide and several hundred metres long, on a rotation every 8-30 years depending upon the build up of dead shoots and woody heather. Although nearly every keeper one speaks to has a different preference for the shape and size of the burnt area. One only has to stand at the top of a glen on a clear day and look out over the miles of moor in all directions to see the many shapes preferred by individual keepers. Sometimes you can spot a mistake, such as where two fires were started parallel to each other and as they burnt the draughts generated brought them together to form an area that looks like a pair of trousers. The strip method has the advantage in that it allows fresh seed to be blown onto the newly burnt area from the older heather either side.

Regeneration of a freshly burnt strip will occur primarily from new shoots from the root stock of the burnt heather, although if the area being burnt was very old heather then it will normally occur from seed. This has the disadvantage of taking longer to re-establish itself thus allowing erosion and dominance by more invasive vegetation. If you examine a burnt area one year later it is easy to see the difference in growth between seed and new shoots, the latter providing a food source a year or more before the germinated seed.

The heat generated by a fire stimulates seed germination and encourages shoot regeneration, however if the fire becomes too hot it will also destroy the humus layer and with it essential nutrients. The heat of the fire is governed by the age of the heather and the conditions on the day. Very mature heather, for example, which reaches higher than the top of your wellington boot, will have a greater ratio of wood to green material and will consequently burn hotter and destroy more vegetation.

THE PRACTICALITIES OF BURNING

It is hot, rather smelly, and it makes your eyes water. Heather burning is a pyromaniac's dream. It can take place between October 1st and April 15th, although most burning takes place in early spring. A team of three or four people is usually all that is required and a miniature fire engine on an Argo is a real advantage. The fire is lit upwind of a fire break, the distance to the fire break will vary according to the wind speed on the day - a strong wind will mean a shorter burn - but should be in excess of 100 metres. The face of the fire should be between 15 and 30 metres wide and, as the fire progresses towards the fire break, fire beaters should be used to control the edges of the fire and ensure that it does not exceed this width. As one fire reaches its end the squad can leave one person to make sure the fire is out and then go and start another. This goes on throughout the day and is very hard work. On a good day a team can light 10-20 fires, and one unlucky soul will have to stay up most of the night to watch the burnt areas and extinguish any fires that may re-ignite.

It is advisable to burn across slopes or downhill as fires tend to be drawn uphill which can lead to control being lost. There are also certain areas of moorland where burning should be avoided; for instance, burning on a steep slope will lead to erosion and burning near fire resistant species such as moor-grass and bracken can lead to dominance by those species.

Heather cutting, using a brush cutter or chain swipes on the back of a tractor, can be used as an alternative to burning in areas where burning would be difficult, such as close to forestry. Although more expensive than burning and not as good, as it does not stimulate seed germination or clean up the ground, it can be a useful alternative when the weather conditions are not right for burning or if the ground is so wet that a fire would not burn well.

REARING AND RELEASING GROUSE

It seems that the generally accepted view is that grouse cannot be reared and released successfully - rubbish!! It can be done and it has been done. As long ago as 1906, the Committee of Inquiry on grouse disease, headed by Lord Lovat, conducted experiments on rearing grouse in captivity and concluded that 'there is little doubt that it might be successfully developed on commercial lines'. Since then, however, very few people have continued the experiments and it is only recently that a gamekeeper in Shropshire has achieved success. Neil Wainwright's interest in grouse arose through his love of falconry and when he moved to Shropshire, as a pheasant keeper, he was fortunate enough to have a few grouse on the estate. Unfortunately the moor was not managed and their numbers dwindled, chiefly through predation and habitat loss, until one day whilst walking the hills he noticed that they were gone. There was no sign of their presence, no droppings, no feathers, nothing.

That was nearly fourteen years ago and the existence of grouse on the moor today is testament to his tenacity and enthusiasm. Undeterred by advice from so called experts that rearing and releasing grouse was not possible, he embarked upon a breeding programme and, through trial and error, succeeded. His first job was to improve the habitat which had suffered through lack of management to the extent that there was very little young heather to sustain a grouse population. A programme of heather burning over several years restored the habitat and then all that was needed were some grouse.

Although in Lord Lovat's experiments brooding grouse eggs under chickens had proved unsuccessful, Neil obtained some eggs from the north of Scotland, a journey that involved an 1,100 mile round trip with three broody bantams, and successfully hatched them. Bantams often do not take to grouse chicks, as discovered by Lord Lovat, and kill them on hatching. Whether this is because young grouse tend to creep, rather than walk upright, so making the foster mother think they are injured, is not known. However it is a problem which arises.

There is one major problem that has to be overcome when rearing grouse for release - diet. As mentioned in the section on disease, the grouse has two caecam or blind guts which are used to help digest the nutritionally poor heather. A young grouse will start eating heather from day one, mixed with high protein insects for the first three weeks of its life, and the caecum will grow to enable it to eat large amounts of heather and extract the nutrients from it. If a young grouse is reared on high protein pellets the caecum, and indeed the rest of the guts, do not develop enough to enable the mature grouse to live on a diet of heather alone and so when released will die from starvation. Therefore to release grouse succesfully they must have access to heather from day one, although high protein chick crumbs can take the place of insects.

The initial batch of grouse reared by the bantams were placed on the hill in pens and soon formed into coveys when released. Though they did not survive the winter, being picked off by foxes one by one, it was a small success. The problem seemed to be that the birds raised by bantams were not 'streetwise' and without grouse as parents were not educated for survival in the wild. Also, as there were so few released the incidence of predation was going to be much higher. In order to produce more birds the following year all the grouse hatched were kept as a breeding stock. As they were not going to be released they could be fed on a diet of heather and pheasant pellets, although now maintainance and breeder pellets for grouse are available from Roslin Nutrition Ltd, Midlothian.

The eggs produced were then placed in incubators and, when hatched, kept for the first week under heater lights on a fine mesh floor. The latter seems to stop them eating their own droppings which can lead to disease. After that they are transferred outside into Rupert Brooders, an old fashioned but effective heated brooder, attached to an outside run. Here they have access to as much heather as they can eat and once they are four weeks old, and no longer need the heaters, they are transferred to pens on the hill until they are ready for release. Using this method Neil has repopulated the moor and the released grouse have survived the winters and bred successfully.

Whilst rearing and releasing grouse is a very useful method to reintroduce grouse where previously there were none, it should not be seen as an alternative to good grouse moor management. It would be a shame if the grouse moors went the way of lowland pheasant shoots where rearing and releasing has replaced good husbandry in providing a harvestable' surplus of game.

GROUSE COUNTS

Grouse counts are a way of assessing the numbers of grouse on a moor in spring and prior to the start of the shooting season. This helps to calculate the number of grouse that can be shot during the season whilst still leaving a good breeding population. Prior to the 1950's, before the methods of counting grouse were devised, the first indication a moor owner had of the number of grouse on the moor was on the first day of the season when they were flying over the butts, or not as the case may be. This was hardly satisfactory when

trying to organize shooting days, guests, or let days. Even now, because the counts are not undertaken until mid to late July, it is quite late before the plans for the season can be finalized and last minute cancellations are always a huge disappointment. Having said that the counts are not the only indication of grouse population. The worm counts carried out during the previous season will give an indication of the health of the grouse and the number of grouse left after the season will provide a pointer to the number of grouse that can

his dog will traverse in six or eight parallel passes starting on the downhill slope. The dog, ranging either side of the keeper, will point any grouse allowing them to be counted as they flush. This will also allow an accurate picture to be built up of the ratio of old birds to young, brood sizes, and pairs that failed, through predation, weather, or other misfortune, to raise a brood. From this number it is possible to work out how many grouse can be shot on that beat that year. Not necessarily by extrapolating the results but by comparing the counts from previous years to what was shot that season.

be expected to breed the next year. This, combined with the weather during the critical hatching period and the size of the broods, will give a reasonable idea of what is on the moor.

Counts are carried out using dogs, preferably pointers or setters, in July when the young grouse are strong flyers. The best time of day is in the early morning when the scent is good and it is not too warm for the dogs or the grouse. There are two kinds of count, a block count and a transect count. The former will give a more accurate picture of the moor from year to year, whilst the latter, though less accurate, will provide a better estimate of the moor as a whole.

Block counts are carried out each year in exactly the same place. The block is a large area of moorland measuring one kilometre squared (250 acres) which the keeper and

Transect counts cover the same amount of ground but rather than walking over a block the keeper walks a line, normally from butt 2, out to the start of the drive before returning on a line 150 metres parallel to the first to come back to butt 8. This can be done for each drive on the beat and, although it is not as accurate as a block count, will give a good indication of what can be shot that season.

Counts can also be undertaken in spring to assess the number of breeding pairs on the moor, this will give an indication how they have come through the winter but not how many there will be in August. With all counts it is inadvisable to regard the results as totally accurate! There have been many pleasant surprises on the first day of the season after poor counts a few weeks before, especially if there was hot weather.

CONCLUSION

Although this is not a comprehensive picture of the role of the gamekeeper in grouse moor management it does, I hope, show that their contribution is pivotal to the success of the grouse moor, not only in conserving grouse stocks but also in preserving the ecologically rich habitat that benefits so many other moorland dwellers.

THE
SPORTING SEASON

FALCONRY

Although the art of falconry is steeped in history and, along with hunting, is one of the oldest recorded field sports, there is little clear evidence of when grouse hawking started. Game hawking has been around for centuries with partridge and pheasant as the most common quarry, although quarry species were never restricted to just game. Heron-hawking and kite-hawking are just two examples of discontinued practices that were, in their day, considered to be the supreme art of hawking. Today grouse hawking, using a peregrine tiercel or falcon, is undoubtedly the classic form of game hawking and is also the most difficult.

The difficulty lies not only in the handling of the dog and the falcon, which, for those of us who have trouble working one dog let alone a pair of pointers and a falcon, is daunting enough. It is also a problem to find a moor on which to fly these birds as the returns from grouse shooting are so high. So now hawking tends to be on the more marginal ground where the fluctuations of the grouse population are greater.

Grouse hawking is a team sport, where the dog, the falcon and the falconer have to work together if they are to succeed. The dogs, usually English pointers and setters, work ahead of the falconer quartering the ground into the wind. When the dog goes on point the falconer removes the hood over the falcon's head and releases her into the wind. She will then climb into the wind, whilst her presence will keep the grouse sitting tightly. The falconer will work his way round the grouse so that he 'heads the point' in other words he is facing the pointer and the grouse are between him and the dog. This allows him to flush the grouse downwind so that the falcon is also stooping downwind and thus able to accelerate quickly.

The falcon by this stage will be nothing but a speck above the falconer's head, hanging in the wind, watching the ground and waiting for the grouse to flush. She will know from experience that the falconer is going to flush the prey and so will position herself so that she can catch the grouse whilst she is still in a steep stoop. If she wanders too far from the falconer her stoop will be too shallow and will end up

tail chasing the grouse. Once she is in position the falconer instructs the dogs to flush the grouse which will, hopefully, turn downwind. The falcon, seeing the grouse, turns and stoops. This is a remarkable sight and over so quickly you have to see it several times before you can take it all in. The falcon stoops almost vertically to gain maximum acceleration over a short distance, and as the grouse moves away the angle of stoop gradually changes so that by the time it hits the grouse it is almost in level flight. The speed is incredible and it is over in a blur, sometimes with the falcon and grouse bound together falling into the heather, other times the falcon will miss.

The falcon will flatten out its stoop before contact so that should it miss its target it can throw itself up above the quarry to regain dominance and to position itself for another stoop.

For a bird that lives on the ground and prefers to walk rather than fly, the speed and agility of a grouse is remarkable. In level flight their acceleration is greater than a falcon's and over a short distance the grouse will outfly a falcon, however grouse are used to short bursts of flight followed by a rest so that after a 500 metres tail chase a tenacious falcon will often catch its prey.

'OVER DOGS' OR DOGGING, AND WALKED-UP GROUSE

Early sportsmen, wishing to partake of the pleasures of grouse shooting, had a formidable task ahead and none but the keenest sportsman would undertake the difficult journey north. In the 18th century a mail coach journey between London and Edinburgh could take three days, and then there was the problem of reaching the Highlands and the more remote moors from there. It was not until the 19th century that transport became easier and grouse shooting became fashionable. Even then, the Edinburgh Mail took nearly 43 hours to complete the journey which was divided into twenty-eight stages with the team of four horses being changed at each stage, a feat that could be carried out in less than a minute. Thus 112 horses would be required for the whole route and, considering there were 30 stage coaches leaving London for Edinburgh, every day, the logistics were colossal.

The discomfort of the journey was not all they had to endure. In the early part of the 19th century the quality of the available lodgings often left much to be desired. Shooting lodges were not the grand affairs they are today, and in the more remote

areas, after a day's sport, the return to a lodge or inn before nightfall was impossible, resulting in the sportsman having to accept hospitality in a shepherd's bothy.

The grouse shooting season had been set by an Act of Parliament in 1773 and, as it came into season earlier than other game birds, the added attraction of combining grouse shooting with stalking and fishing made the trip north all the more worthwhile. In the early 1800's grouse shooting was almost always over pointers and setters. The sportsman at that time only had the muzzleloader at his disposal and so was unable to load quickly enough to make driven grouse worthwhile. Because he only had one shot, followed by a fairly lengthy reloading procedure, each shot had to count and so dogs were needed that were able to mark the birds and allow the gun to get into position before they were flushed. The pointer was derived from a cross between a Spanish pointer and a foxhound whilst the setter was a breed of spaniel, known as the English spaniel, that had been trained to facilitate the taking of game with nets. Thus the dog had to sit or set whilst the net was drawn over the covey of grouse or partridge. Its smaller relation, the springer spaniel, was used to find and spring the game.

It is a real pleasure to watch a pointer at work, ranging over the moor scenting the air for grouse, which, once located, will turn in their direction to go on point. This is a tremendously exciting moment as you know there is a grouse close by (although some dogs do seem to have a predilection for pointing larks). Then, as the two guns approach, he will begin to 'draw' towards the grouse, creeping slowly towards it (or them). If the scent is good he can draw over fifty yards, with the excitement mounting at every step. The guns will keep up with the dog as he gets closer to the grouse, changing direction as he changes direction, all the time anticipating the flush of the birds. If the grouse are running ahead he may draw several hundred yards and the

tension can be almost unbearable. Once the grouse are actually located then the command to flush can be given and in a flash the birds are up and away.

On large areas of moorland it is normal practice to run a brace of pointers at the same time, each with its own territory, quartering the ground individually but aware of the other's presence. As soon as one goes on point the other will cease working the ground and back its partner up from the flank or the rear, remaining there until the birds are flushed.

This type of shooting tends to take place in the early part of the season before the birds become too wild and flighty. Last century, longer heather was favoured by keepers as the grouse would sit tighter and were easier to approach. This was before it was realised that tall heather had no nutritional value to the grouse and therefore adversely affected numbers.

Much of the excitement of shooting over pointers and setters is in the anticipation of a flush once the dogs have gone on point. That, and watching the dogs working, provides an enormous amount of pleasure.

The fact that it takes place in some of the most beautiful landscape in the country is a real bonus. Luckily we no longer have to endure the hardships our predecessors had to tolerate and, at the end of a good day's sport, can be whisked off the hill in a four-wheel-drive vehicle, back to a warm bath and a restorative whisky.

Walked up shooting, as opposed to 'over dogs' or dogging, has become more prevalent since the advent of driven sport. This has the keeper, beat keepers and their dogs, usually labradors or spaniels, interspersed between the line of guns and the whole party then marches abreast across the moor. This has developed following the advent of driven shooting which requires quicker retrievers than the traditional form of grouse shooting and so these types of dogs are now more popular. One of life's certainties, like death and taxes, is that there will be at least one unruly dog in the line. The last thing one wants to see after scrambling up the steep sides of a gully, with legs like jelly and one's heart pounding like a sledgehammer, is a black labrador effortlessly running across the heather sixty yards out flushing grouse that disappear over the horizon. If you are really unfortunate there will be two such dogs in the line, one of whom will belong to the keeper and any helpful suggestions concerning dog training which you direct at him will lead to a particularly barren spell,

over hard ground, with no grouse. On one particular day in Scotland, the area we were shooting was heaving with mountain hares, we saw three for every grouse, and the keeper's dog chased most of them. I initially mistook the keeper's shouting for words of encouragement for every time it gave chase he was heard to bellow "Run, Run". This seemed to be a very peculiar practice and, keen as I am to witness all countrysports, I would rather restrict coursing to the withers of Altcar. It was several hours before my ear, becoming attuned to the Gallic tongue, discerned that the dog was called Rum and the fierce bellows were a futile attempt to arrest the pursuit. By lunchtime I was tempted to ask him how much his dog was worth, give him the money and then shoot it. Indeed, by 3.00pm, nothing would have given me greater pleasure than adding two labradors to the bag for there was another miscreant in the line, this time belonging to one of the guns, who decided it would be more fun to leave her master and come down to our end of the line to add moral support to Rum's endeavors.

Using labradors and spaniels there is little warning of a covey of grouse bursting from the heather. In an ideal world the dogs should hunt close to the guns allowing a little time between the whirring of the wings, as the grouse lift out of the heather, and the same birds disappearing out of shot. When one is standing on level ground and prepared for the burst of activity this can seem quite a long time, however when on a slope, in thick heather, with a gale buffeting your back the moment has vanished in a millisecond.

Sadly the traditional practice of shooting grouse over pointers is becoming increasingly rare. As driven shooting became more popular, and the rents increased, moors that were used purely for walked-up shooting diminished. There are still a few enclaves left, such as in Caithness, where it is possible to savour the delights of watching good dogs working the ground, and to anyone who has not experienced this pleasure I would strongly recommend it. There is however a certain amount of walked-up shooting taking place each year, notably on moors which don't have sufficient grouse for a driven day, but are happy to bring in some income by letting a few days of this type.

'Carting' grouse deserves a brief mention. It is a method of shooting grouse which was brought to my attention by the Duke of Northumberland and his own words describe it perfectly :

"I came across this method in the Edwardian writer, Abel Chapman's 'Border Reflections'. When the grouse become too wary to walk-up, Chapman lurked beside a moving horse and cart, which could get much closer to the unsuspecting birds. At the critical moment he would jump around the corner of the cart, trying not to startle or shoot the horse, and bag his brace without more ado. The modern grouse is similarly susceptible to motor vehicles, and the same method can be applied with, say, a Landrover. The purist will walk beside the vehicle which is being driven by an accomplice, but I tend to do it on my own, when I need a bird or two for dinner, or I need a first grouse for a young shot with short legs. The problem then, is to approach the birds, get out of the car, load the gun and shoot the grouse before it disapppears over the far horizon. Winding down the window and blasting off from the driver's seat is frowned on, and in any case leaves a terrible ringing in the ears even if you remember to put the earphones on. If the bird is flying it is almost impossible to swing and fire without bashing the gun on the window frame. Carting, or more accurately Landrovering, is a fine sport, but there are dangers; never try to save time by having a loaded gun in the car, and always remember to apply the handbrake before you leap out."

DRIVEN GROUSE

It is a magical time, that period before the grouse arrive when one can lean against the front of the butt, elbows resting on the damp heather, and view the scene which stretches out into the distance. It is a time for absorbing every detail, the colour of the heather, the distant hills tinged blue in the cool light, the misty valleys below. Although a butt facing a steep incline gives less time to see the birds and, some may say, provides more exciting shooting, my preference is always for a butt with a view, one where I can follow the beaters approach, the distant flash of their white flags the only indication of their presence, and watch the coveys of grouse moving before them. There is nothing to beat the majestic stone butt, half sunk in the ground, and capped with heather or bilberry. They are a joy to behold. The

anticipation, followed by the excitement as the grouse burst into view is one of the rich pleasures of life; a combination of weather, heather and feather, that can make a perfect day.

Driven grouse shooting is a relative newcomer to the sporting scene when compared to hunting or falconry. For its emergence as a sport we owe an enormous debt to the English gunmakers for it was the development of the shotgun and ammunition which made it possible. Although it was a Bristol plumber by the name of William Watts who, in 1782, developed the method of making perfectly spherical lead shot without which the chance of getting a reasonable pattern through any gun would have been impossible. He did this by dropping molten lead, from a height, through sieves into water, the same method that is still used today.

Advances continued to be made throughout the next century but it was between 1860 and 1880 when most of the designs for shotguns as we know them today were developed. In 1860 George Henry Daw introduced the first breechloading English shotgun, although it had been developed by a Frenchman, Lefaucheux, and first seen at the Great Exhibition at Crystal Palace in 1851. It was now possible to reload quickly using a

cartridge rather then the lengthy procedure of muzzleloading. In 1864 smokeless gunpowder was developed making it possible, for the first time, to see if you had hit the bird you were aiming at. Prior to that the old black powder produced such a cloud of smoke that all was obscured from view. The new powder also allowed the discharge of the second barrel as you would still be able to see the covey of grouse.

There were other factors, too, which increased the popularity of the sport. The advent of the railways made the grouse moors much more accessible, especially those in Scotland. After Queen Victoria leased Balmoral in 1848, and subsequently bought the estate in 1852, it became

fashionable to indulge in country sports. A year later saw the launch of that illustrious tome on all matters to do with countrysports, The Field, which played an important role in the development of the sport as, in addition to grouse reports during the season, it furnished its readers with information on grouse shooting and management. The popularity of driven grouse was further enhanced by the royal patronage of Edward VII, something that would have been unheard of a century before when shooting was not considered a proper pastime for the aristocracy.

It was also a far cry from the criticism levelled at driven grouse shooting when it first started at the beginning of the 1800's. Muzzleloaders were more conducive to shooting over dogs than driven shooting as reloading took such a long time. Despite this inconvenience driven grouse shooting did start before the introduction of the breech-loading shotgun and this is, perhaps, what provided the impetus for its development. The Bishop of Durham's Horsley Moor had drives laid out by 1803 and the butts were still in the same position a century later. This new sport was, in many circles, considered to be unsportsmanlike despite the fact that the skill involved in shooting a fast flying grouse with muzzleloader using black powder was enormous. In those early days three brace per drive was considered a large bag although by the mid 1800's larger bags were being obtained, mainly through better organisation, and a gentleman called Horatio Ross even managed to shoot 82 grouse for 82 shots on his 82nd birthday with a muzzleloader.

So by the 1870's the sport of driven grouse shooting was firmly established and the bags started to rise. In 1888 Lord Walsingham shot 1,070 grouse to his own gun at Blubberhouse Moor in Yorkshire. The development of driven grouse shooting also created a whole new job market, rather than two or three people shooting over dogs there was suddenly a need for beaters, flankers and pickers-up. The clever marketing ploy by the best London gunmakers who persuaded their clients that they could shoot more grouse if they had a pair of guns increased their profits and created the need for cartridge boys and loaders. I have probably spent more time as a loader than actually shooting grouse and, whilst nothing can compare to the thrill of shooting, loading does provide all the elements of a day's shooting bar pulling the trigger. There are three sins a loader must never commit: running out of cartridges during a drive, clanging barrels whilst changing guns, and handing back an empty gun having forgotten to load it in the excitement of the moment. There should be a fourth which was experienced by a friend of mine during his first drive as a loader. The first covey came towards the guns, jinking in the wind, and the gun, who was an experienced shot, took the first two in front of the butt. When he turned to exchange guns he saw his loader, overcome with excitement, shooting another two out of the back!

The role of the keeper, too, has changed beyond all recognition since the introduction of driven shooting. On a double gun grouse day today there will be nearly 40 people in supporting roles to the nine guns, all having to be organised by him. His role as moorland manager too has changed. Driven shooting requires a far higher population of grouse and so management techniques need to be different. Early gamekeepers on dogging moors had to do very little in the way of predator control and heather burning was left to the shepherds. The gamekeeper's primary role was to provide game for his master's table.

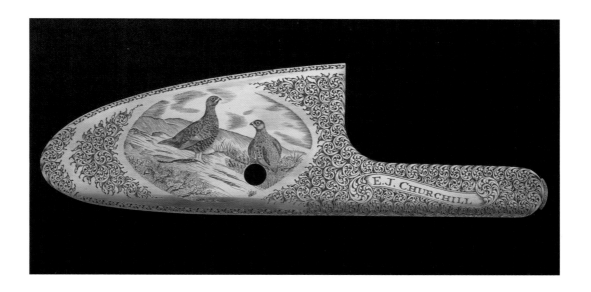

On the opposite page are the designs I did for the side plates of a pair guns by E. J. Churchill Gunmakers. The guns were the prize in the Game Conservancy Trust's Millennium Draw and made to the winner's specification.

Above are the side plates for No. 1 gun which were engraved by Peter Cusack.

MOORLAND WILDLIFE

INTRODUCTION

I remember the first time I stood in a butt on a moor. It was in Scotland on a rather grey day with low cloud and intermittent drizzle. The heather had lost all its colour and the whole landscape looked dark and uninviting. I wondered what could live in such a harsh and barren landscape seemingly bereft of all life forms, save us and the grouse. The latter were due to expectation rather than visual evidence. In comparison to the lowlands, with their rich diversity of habitat, heather moorland can look bare and bleak, especially on a winter's day in the Highlands. In truth, moorland holds a rich diversity of flora and fauna but it takes time to discover its secrets. I was entranced the first time I saw a mountain hare, and the haunting cry of the curlew never fails to draw my eyes skywards, often at the same time as a covey of grouse fly past my butt. The rich eco-system that has developed on and around moorland owes much to the influence of grouse management. Retaining habitat for such birds as the golden plover and snipe is vital for their survival and gamekeeping, particularly predator control, improves the breeding success of all ground nesting birds. Indeed a survey by the RSPB and The Game Conservancy Trust showed that golden plovers and lapwings were five times as abundant on grouse moors compared with other moors.

This part of the book highlights some of the species to be found on the moor or close to its edges. It is by no means exclusive and the space dedicated to each has no bearing on their density on the moor, rather it is a reflection of my particular fondness for a species.

PTARMIGAN

LAGOPUS MUTUS MILLAISI

A rough translation of the Latin name Lagopus mutus is hairy footed and silent. A delightful name for this rarely seen member of the grouse family. Few, but the most dedicated sportsmen and hill walkers, venture into their harsh domain and trying to spot the birds, with their near perfect camouflage, takes a practiced eye. The most difficult time to see them is when there is just a light covering of snow with bare rocks - then all one can do is hope that their movement will give them away.

Like the mountain hare they change their colouring in winter becoming pure white, except for their dark bill and tail feathers, allowing them to blend into the snowy landscape. The males are distinguishable from the females, at this time of year, by a small black streak running from the bill to the eye. They go through three plumage changes during the year. As the snow begins to clear they begin to change to their spring plumage from late February to early May. From June to September they will have a complete moult renewing their wing and tail feathers and taking on a delicate grey plumage before reverting back to their winter plumage from September to November. The exact timing of the moult will depend on the altitude and areas they inhabit.

Normally found around 3,000ft altitude they are the only bird inhabiting these inhospitable surroundings all year round. In very harsh weather they will seek shelter in rocky corries. The only other creature that can tolerate the extreme weather is the mountain hare.

Although the territories of the ptarmigan and red grouse rarely overlap, their diet is very similar, relying on heather, blaeberry and crowberry for their nutrition. However, the former will resort to anything that can provide sustenance, even pecking at the lichen on rocks.

THE BROWN HARE

LEPUS EUROPAEUS

Although strictly a lowland mammal, they are often found on grouse moors up to an altitude of 2,000 feet. I never tire of drawing hares and had to force myself onto other subjects before they started to dominate this section. Their expressive faces and graceful lines are an artist's dream and it is a real bonus to see one running past the butts. Unfortunately, on moors where louping ill is prevalent hares, as tick hosts, are discouraged. However elsewhere their presence can be plentiful.

The hare has changed little since prehistoric times, as fossilised remains testify. It is a creature steeped in legend and myth, the most notable of which was the association, in the middle ages, of hares with witchcraft, indeed such is the folklore surrounding the hare that there are still many country households that will not have a dead hare in the house. The subject of early man's cave paintings has constantly played a part in art and literature. Aesop's many fables about the hare exhibited a profound knowledge of its character, and Shakespeare regarded the hare, with its rather doleful expression, as a melancholy creature.

The female, or doe, will start to breed from 12 months old and can have as many as four litters in a season. The leverets are born into a 'form', which is a small depression in the ground, but are soon split up and taken, by the mother, to individual hiding places. They are born with their eyes open and a full coat of fur, which is especially useful to early litters which can be caught by a late frost or even snow.

Although the leverets have very little scent they are nevertheless predated upon by foxes and stoats, one reason why the mother separates her brood at an early age. She will, however, vigorously defend her young, even against a fox, using her powerful back legs and sharp claws to repel attack.

The brown hare is a fairly solitary character, except in spring when during courtship they cavort in the open fields, boxing and chasing until mating takes place. Although the doe will have several litters in a year the courtship ritual only seems to take place for the early mating, subsequent matings seem to occur without the display. After mating, the male will retire and take no part in the raising of the family.

CURLEW

NUMENIUS ARQUATA

This distinctive bird with its long down-curved bill is the largest British wader. The resident population spend the autumn and winter in coastal areas where they are joined by others migrating from Scandinavia, the former Baltic States and northwest Russia. The west coast of Britain is a popular area for them although many move over to Ireland and further still to Iceland, the Faroes, and even the West African coast. They are capable of migrating at remarkable altitudes and have been recorded crossing the Himalayas at over 20,000 feet. Their winter food includes ragworms, lugworms, shrimps, small crabs and shellfish, all of which are readily available in their coastal haunts.

In February and March they will start to abandon their winter feeding grounds and those that do not migrate will leave the coast to breed on open moorland, rough pasture and boggy ground. It is the decline of this type of habitat which has led to the reduction in curlew numbers. Factors such as increased grazing pressure, drainage, forestry and predation have all contributed making grouse moors an increasingly important habitat. Here they benefit from the protection afforded to them by gamekeepers. They will nest on or near a tussock or mound, newly burnt areas being especially popular. The preservation of this habitat and the control of predators means that curlews are twice as common here than on unmanaged moors.

They will start to lay a clutch of four eggs in April and, like the golden plover, incubation is shared by both parents. The newly hatched chicks have uncurved bills and their diet is similar to that of the young grouse, feeding mainly on insects. The adult curlew's summer diet consists mainly of earthworms and leather-jackets although beetles, caterpillars and spiders will all be eaten with relish. When the young become fully grown in July they will start to leave the high ground and return to the estuaries although they still can be seen on the moors in August.

Except in Northern Ireland, where they are still legal quarry, they are fully protected. It is a shame then that the introduction of the right to roam, by a government that has little thought for the consequences of such a policy, will undoubtedly affect the breeding success of this shy bird. Repeated disturbance of ground nesting waders, which are often more sensitive than grouse, will lead to them abandoning their eggs and chicks.

GOLDEN PLOVER

PLUVIALIS APRICARIA

The British breeding population of this beautifully coloured bird owes its survival to grouse moor management. Whilst the majority of golden plovers arrive from Iceland and Scandinavia in October and spend the winter months feeding on lowland and coastal areas, the resident population, which consists of under 30,000 pairs, breed mainly on moorland. As a ground nesting bird they can suffer from high levels of predation during the critical breeding period which is why they are more successful on grouse moors compared with other moors. A few, however, can be seen nesting on Dartmoor which are the most southerly birds of their species in the world.

This is another example of gamekeeping helping other species to flourish as predator control is a benefit to all ground nesting birds. The government has proposed that wild bird populations should be indicators of sustainable land use and this clearly shows the sustainability of grouse moor management. The birds lay a clutch of four eggs from the end of April and both parents will share the incubation. The young birds mature quickly and are able to fly at four weeks old and are fully independent a week or so later.

In winter the golden plover has a golden spotted breast with a white belly. Their summer plumage, which is attained in the spring moult between mid-March and mid-April, is very distinctive with a black mask and bib. Apart from the resident birds, the rest migrate back to Scandinavia and Iceland from the end of February. The majority arrive in Iceland in May where they are the harbinger of summer. "The Golden Plover has arrived to sing away the snow," is a prophetic line from an old favourite Icelandic song.

Like the lapwing, golden plovers are birds of the fields rather than the mudflats although they can be seen on the grassier stretches of the salt marshes. They do, however, like to visit the mudflats in the evening to bathe and huge flocks of several thousand can sometimes be seen congregating in the evening light around the pools on the flats. As the light fails they will leave in great flights, filling the air with their beautiful plaintive whistle, as they return to the marshes.

Few are shot, despite being on the quarry list between September 1st and January 31st. This may be because on many moors they are a rare sight and fly past unrecognised. When they are seen they will often be in large flocks flying high over the moors, their plaintive piping announcing their presence before they are visible. Their sharply pointed wings give them complete mastery of the air and they are very acrobatic in flight.

LAPWING

VANELLUS VANELLUS

This striking bird is known by various names, each one descriptive of a particular characteristic. The 'lapwing' describes its broad winged flight, the green plover its shimmering feathers and the peewit its distinctive cry. As agricultural practices change, the lapwing's habitat has shrunk causing a collapse in the population in recent years. All the more important, then, that grouse moor management maintains the habitat that many of them favour for breeding. With their absence from most of the lowland areas where they were once common, the contribution of grouse moor management to the national population is enormous. In northern Britain they will start to take up their territories in April and this is when the male undertakes his spectacular display flights. He will slowly rise in the air before suddenly diving down, twisting and turning, whilst making a medley of shrill and unmistakable cries. Like the golden plover and snipe, there is a large migratory influx in winter and a smaller resident breeding population in the summer, and, like all moorland ground nesting birds, they benefit from predator control and habitat preservation.

THE MOUNTAIN HARE

LEPUS TIMIDUS

The most obvious differences between the mountain hare and its lowland cousin are the shorter ears and, in winter, its white coat. It is also smaller and stockier with a slightly different shaped head and a totally white tail, without the familiar black upper parts of the brown hare. Unlike the brown hare, the mountain hare is more gregarious and can often be seen in quite large numbers all year round, this is most obvious if the snow thaws whilst they are still in their winter coat, the tiny white dots on the side of the glen highlighting their presence.

The mountain hare is the only British mammal, apart from the stoat, to become white in winter, the Romans thought that this was because it ate snow! The change starts from mid-October and can vary from individual to individual, some not changing until December, whilst those at lower altitudes may retain some of their brown coat throughout the winter. Like their neighbours on the high slopes, the ptarmigan, they will start to change back to the summer colouring from mid-February. The other common name for the mountain hare is the blue hare, so named because during this transition the two different colourings can give a blue appearance.

As well as having to keep a wary eye open for the same four legged predators that look upon the brown hare as a meal, the mountain hare has to watch out for the stoop of the eagle, which regard it as a choice morsel. It is, perhaps, for this reason that the mountain hare, unlike the brown hare, will use thick cover, or even a rocky outcrop, to remain concealed from above.

Because of the climate and the shorter summers, the mountain hare will not have as many litters as the brown hare, stopping around August time. This will give the young time to mature before the harsh winter sets in. Its diet, too, is more restricted as the moorland does not provide such an extensive array of vegetation but, as with brown hares, it will use refection (eating their own droppings) to fully extract the nutrients from their high cellulose diets.

There is also another species of mountain hare Lepus timidus hibernicus, which is a distinct subspecies found only in Ireland.

RAVEN

CORVUS CORAX

There are numerous stories of the raven, in exchange for the gralloch, guiding stalkers to their target and the cry of the raven echoing off the crags, can stir the atavistic senses. These magnificent birds live in the same territory year after year and will often be encountered on the higher moors where there are plentiful nesting areas amongst the steep crags. In flight, their wingspan is nearly as big as that of a buzzard and they appear to dive and roll in their windy environment for pure pleasure. Their principal food is dead sheep and, during the stalking season, the gralloch, although they do eat small mammals, frogs, lizards and insects. Generally the population is increasing.

RED DEER

CERVUS ELAPHUS

This, the largest of our wild mammals, was originally a woodland dwelling animal. As the ancient forests were cleared the red deer gradually moved to more inhospitable places and now the largest populations are found in the Highlands of Scotland. They also populate various parts of England but rarely where grouse are in evidence.

It is estimated that there are around 300,000 red deer in Scotland, a trebling of the population in the last four decades, and stalking is a major part of the Scottish economy in the more remote areas. There is a conflict between deer and grouse which often leads to moorland being used for one or the other. Keen stalking lairds find grouse a nuisance as they not only compete for food but also can wreck a stalk. The alarm call of a grouse, disturbed whilst stalking a herd, will often spook the deer and waste many hours of crawling through damp heather. In years when the grouse population is high this can make stalking almost impossible.

On grouse moors the deer compete with the grouse for food and are regarded by many grouse keepers as vermin. This problem is becoming more acute with the damage caused by the heather beetle which is reducing the winter food supply and therefore the carrying capacity of the moor. This is exacerbated by the fact that in Scotland the underlying rock strata affects the soil fertility and therefore the nutritional value of the heather is generally less productive than England. This is why you will generally see much bigger stags with more impressive heads on Exmoor in the West Country. So the competition for food can lead to conflict between deer and grouse and red deer will not be welcome on those moors that are managed for grouse. All deer species can pose a further problem in that they are hosts for ticks and as such can spread louping ill, so in areas where this disease is prevalent all mammals will be discouraged.

ROE DEER

CAPREOLUS CAPREOLUS

It came as a bit of a surprise to me to see these predominately woodland dwellers on moorland. Both times were in Scotland whilst stalking. The first was whilst roe stalking in woodland next to the moor. We had been through the wood and emerged at the top where the moor started and where we had a good viewpoint down to the wood where we hoped the roe would come out in early evening to graze. We lay in the heather and waited, and waited. Nothing. The light was failing quickly so we decided to abandon our task and return home to the log fire and a glass of whisky. However, when we got up and looked behind us there on the tops, silhouetted against the evening sky were a buck and a doe. Further along the ridge there was another.

The next day I was up onto the hill after a stag. The first stalk was successful and achieved fairly quickly so we embarked upon another. There was a herd of stags laid up below the ridge in a dip that allowed us to approach from above. A long crawl through the heather and we were in position, albeit a rather uncomfortable one on a downhill slope, waiting for the chosen beast to stand up. It was a relatively mild October day with a gentle breeze that was unfortunately insufficient to keep that bane of the Highlands, the Scottish midge, at

bay. They always seem to regard me rather fondly, taking the trouble to single me out from any companions to feast relentlessly. I do not begrudge them a meal, I just wish their legacy wasn't so irritating. We waited 20 minutes, which equated to about 40 midge bites, before we spotted a roe doe, which must have scented us, racing up the glen towards the stags. They immediately rose to their feet and bolted giving no chance of a shot.

Talking to the stalkers I was assured that roe are fairly common on the moor. Whether this is because there is insufficient territory in the woodlands or because they actually prefer to be on the moor I do not know, but, even at the loss of a successful stalk, it is always a pleasure to see roe deer. They are, for me, the prettiest and most elegant of our native species and one of the most difficult to draw correctly. I think this is because of the eyes. Last year I spent three months sculpting a life size roe buck and discovered during the course of many dissections that the eye points 45% forwards and about 9% downwards. Unlike some of the mounted heads I have seen, with the eyes mounted on the side of the head, the roe does not have the ability to see behind it, relying instead on its other senses to alert it of danger approaching from that direction.

SNIPE

GALLINAGO GALLINAGO

The occasional snipe appearing during a grouse drive is a fine bonus, causing shouts of warning to the gun towards whose butt the bird is heading. They often pass overhead unseen, such is the concentration devoted to the possible approach of grouse. For me, they are always a worthy target and one that, more often than not, highlights the inadequacies in my marksmanship. We all have a mental library of our most memorable shots and, although I can remember exceptional grouse drives, I have yet to shoot a truly outstanding grouse. A snipe, however, shot during one of the best grouse drives I have ever had, is in my top three, alongside a teal shot nearly fifteen years ago and a woodcock from this season. I had seen it flush from a reed bed 200 yards away and watched jinking and rising as it moved towards the butts. I ducked down low in the butt and watched it through the stems of heather capping the butt. It carried on rising and moving

in my direction, by the time it was over me it was at the height of a west country pheasant and I was somewhat surprised when it fell to my first shot.

Although the driven snipe will often be at a good altitude it is the walked-up birds that are often the most testing. Their jinking flight can make fools of us all, and if you are not constantly alert then they will often be out of range before the gun is mounted.

The snipe we see on the moor in August will be resident birds that have bred in tussocks of grass near moorland bogs that summer. Migratory birds do not arrive from Scandinavia and Iceland until September or October. They feed in boggy areas where their bills can probe the soft earth in search of worms. Their bills are similar in design to the woodcock in that the top of the bill near the end is formed from hard skin with nerve endings close to the surface to detect the worms beneath the surface. This is why the bill of a dead bird tends to wrinkle at the end after a few hours.

The snipe population has fallen dramatically since the 1950's when drainage and land reclamation for agriculture and forestry led to a severe loss of habitat. Grouse moor management has certainly helped maintain a resident breeding population through predator control and by providing suitable habitat in the form of bog flushes.

THE PREDATORS

Grouse feature prominently on many a moorland predator's diet and much of the gamekeeper's time is spent trying to prevent the former becoming a meal for the latter. Whilst most of the mammalian predators are not protected, and can therefore be controlled, there is an increasing problem with birds of prey. It is a problem that needs to be resolved before lasting damage is done to the fragile ecosystems that exist in the uplands.

The fox, stoat, and weasel are the main four legged predators which eat grouse. The latter are amazing killers for their size and will kill a hen on the nest. Rats, and occasionally mink, will sometimes prey on grouse if the opportunity exists but are not a major threat. All have been mentioned in more detail in the chapter on predator control so here I will deal with those predators that are protected, namely, the raptors.

In the moorland food chain the raptors are at the top and consequently their numbers will affect the populations of all the other creatures on the moor. Perhaps the only bird of prey that is regarded with a degree of benevolence by gamekeepers is the tiny merlin, the smallest falcon in the UK. Small birds, such as meadow pipits and skylarks,

form the major part of their diet although they will also tackle small waders like dunlin and snipe. The preservation of heather moorland is vital for its survival and its future is inexorably linked to that of the grouse. Forestry planting and overgrazing both pose a threat. The former not only destroys the merlin's habitat but also encourages the forest dwelling sparrowhawk which preys on the merlin.

All of the other raptors, with the exception of the red kite and kestrel, prey on grouse and, if their numbers become too high, will affect the viability of the moor, which is what happened at Langholm during the Joint Raptor Study. What compounds this tragedy is that it is not only the grouse that suffer. Many other birds and mammals in the delicate moorland ecosystem are adversely affected once the keepers are no longer present to control crows and foxes. In the longer term this will also have an adverse affect on the numbers of birds of prey.

The worst offenders, by far, are the hen harrier and the peregrine falcon. During the period of study at Langholm the breeding pairs of hen harriers rose from 2 to 21 and peregrines from 2 to 6. Ironically it is because grouse moors are

THE RAPTORS

Clockwise from top left:

Hen harrier
Golden eagle
Sparrowhawk
Goshawk
Merlin
Kestrel
Peregrine
Buzzard

well managed that hen harriers can proliferate. On unmanaged moors, where foxes are abundant, the ground nesting harrier does not stand much of a chance as the fox will soon find their rather smelly nest site and eat the eggs or chicks. As most grouse shots will know, what happened at Langholm was a tragedy. A very productive grouse moor was, over a period of five years, decimated by a population boom in raptors to such an extent that it was no longer viable as a moor and shooting ceased. Langholm was the first scientific study to show that raptors were a problem on grouse moors. Most grouse keepers could have attested to that fact beforehand but if there is ever going to be any hope of resolving the issue it is essential to have scientific fact to support common sense. Unfortunately, during the study period, Langholm also suffered a severe loss of heather due to overgrazing and the RSPB attributed the decline in grouse numbers to this and not the raptor predation.

What has happened since then is just as tragic on two counts. Firstly, since Langholm nothing has been resolved on the issue of control of raptors, with the result that many other grouse moors are reaching that critical state where shooting may cease altogether. Secondly, since grouse shooting ceased, and the gamekeepers were laid off, the other moorland creatures have suffered a collapse in numbers. The reasons are not difficult to find - 21 hen harrier nest sites in 1997 produced 108 hen harriers which, if each killed three small birds a day, would result in over 100,000 small birds being killed in a year. During the breeding season it was estimated that grouse chicks made up 37% of the hen harriers' diet, the remainder comprising meadow pipits, skylarks, lapwings, curlews and all of the other ground nesting birds found on the moor. The result being that their numbers have fallen dramatically. The sad thing is that these hen harrier numbers are not sustainable and since gamekeepers were removed from the moor their population has also crashed with only seven pairs breeding successfully in 2000. Unfortunately this has not led to an increase in other bird species as foxes, crows, and other predators have moved in.

There are no areas in the United Kingdom where man's influence is absent and consequently there is no such thing as a natural balance. If we are to maintain a diverse and balanced environment then we must control the predators that are at the top of the food chain. To allow their populations to grow, unchecked, will lead to a dramatic downfall in other bird species and will be of little benefit to themselves. No one is advocating total elimination of these magnificent birds, just a balanced approach to ensure that their numbers do not rise at the expense of other species.

CONCLUSION

There are many other species of wildlife on the moor, almost too numerous to mention. Indeed, this whole section could be a book in itself. Birds such as the meadow pipit, skylark, ring ouzel and the rare dotterel can all be present on the moor. Whilst the greenshank, dunlin, and golden plover have over 90% of their European population in Britain, the majority of which will nest on moorland.

Mention, too, should be made of amphibians such as frogs and toads, and the abundant insect life, so important to the survival of young grouse, and important contributors to the rich and diverse habitat on which so many creatures depend. Grouse moors contribute significantly to the biodiversity of the uplands and maintaining this balance is of the utmost importance.

LIFE ON
THE MOORLAND FRINGES

Whilst moorland wildlife thrives from the management of the grouse moors, there are other species, living on the fringes of the moor, which also benefit. Here is a brief mention of some of the game species living on the edge of the moor and whose future is linked to good gamekeeping practice and habitat management.

BLACK GROUSE

TETRAO TETRIX

There are few more unusual sights in the uplands than the black grouse lek, where the males fan out their lyre-shaped tail, drop their wings, puff out their neck feathers and strut. They start before dawn when all you can see in the murky light is the puffball of white feathers on their bottoms and hear the cooing noise, similar to that heard in a dovecote. It is a remarkable sight, all the more so because they do this for months on end. There is a brief lull in late summer and autumn whilst they are moulting and so not looking their best, but for the rest of the year, irrespective of the weather, or the presence of a grey hen - the female black grouse - the males will gather at the lek site and pose in vain splendour, engaging in occasional mock fights, never serious enough to damage their feathers. In spring, the hens attend the lek regularly in search of the dominant males with whom they will mate. That service fulfilled, the males will play no further role in the breeding process, preferring, instead, to continue with their vain display. The lek site measures around an acre in size and is divided up into small territories, with the dominant males holding the areas closer to the centre.

Black game are generally found at a lower altitude than the red grouse, preferring moorland edges and open forests, but they will frequently overlap. They have suffered a catastrophic population crash in the last decade, dropping from 25,000 to 6,500 in just ten years. Much of this is due to habitat loss and predation, with the result that many moorland owners, in an attempt to halt the decline, will no longer allow them to be shot. Their habitat of choice is often young plantations but they will move on once the overhead cover becomes dense. Clearings in mature forests that allow the regeneration of birch scrub are also popular, and research is being carried out to assess the value of this type of habitat in an attempt to stem the decline.

CAPERCAILLIE

TETRAO UROGALLUS

They are huge, as big as a turkey, and a male approaching in full display is an impressive sight, and one to be wary of, for they will attack intruders into their territory. As their favoured habitat is natural pine forest, as opposed to plantations, they will rarely be seen on open moorland, however, predator control undoubtedly helps this increasingly rare bird. Their population is estimated to be around 3,500, of which only 1,000 are females, and is in danger of repeating what happened in the late 1700's when they became extinct in the British Isles. The main cause of this decline was a combination deforestation, a succession of poor breeding seasons, and a mini ice age. Although shooting would have contributed to its demise it was not a significant factor and it was sportsmen who imported a few birds from Sweden in the early 1800's and successfully re-introduced them in Perthshire. They are now found only north of the River Forth and predator control and habitat preservation are the best methods to preserve this impressive member of the grouse family.

Despite a voluntary ban on shooting capercaillie, instigated and enforced by sportsmen, they have recently been removed from the quarry list. What advantage may consequently be enjoyed by this magnificent bird is uncertain. The ban is contrary to the recommendations of the Biodiversity Action Plan (BAP) Working Group, of which the RSPB is a member, together with The Game Conservancy Trust, Scottish Natural Heritage, Forestry Commission, and landowners. BAP felt that a total ban "would give a disincentive for landowners who wish to be able to shoot capercaillie in the future when the population has recovered." Although sporting interests are not the major motivating factor behind capercaillie conservation, sportsmen's contribution to the caper's future has played a large part in its survival.

WOODCOCK

SCOLOPAX RUSTICOLA

Whilst the grouse holds the title of the king of gamebirds the woodcock, in my view, runs a very close second. My heart is stirred every time I see one and I never tire of watching them flighting to feed against fading evening light. They are primarily a woodland dweller, however they do venture out onto the grassy parts of the moor to feed at night. We do have a small resident population that remain to breed and most birds seen before November will fall into this category. My most unusual sighting was on August 12th when one flew through the butts during a grouse drive. It provided a rare opportunity to observe its flight for some considerable time, normally it is just a brief glimpse as they flit between trees. Areas of woodland close to moors are perfect for these resident birds, providing safety from predators and an ideal habitat to help them breed successfully.

GREY PARTRIDGE

PERDIX PERDIX

It is a rare sight nowadays to see a covey of wild grey partridge bursting over the hedgerows. In the seventies, when I was learning to shoot, we had numerous coveys on the farm in Yorkshire where I was brought up. Sadly, for this, the prettiest of gamebirds, things have changed. Such has been the catastrophic collapse in their numbers over the last 30 years they have now been placed on the vulnerable list, subject to a government biodiversity action plan, with calls to put them on the protected list. The Game Conservancy Trust's research has shown that declining insect population is at the root of the problem and, with the

continuing pressure on farmers to become more efficient, the downward trend is likely to continue. There are a few benevolent estates and farms where insect producing habitat is actively managed to promote their well-being and produce a harvestable surplus. As sportsmen are doing most of the work to preserve the grey partridge, placing it on the protected list would have an adverse effect on its future. What is really needed is a comprehensive reform of the Common Agricultural Policy and, in addition, for more lowland shoots to manage their ground to boost the number of insects and keep predators under control.

One area where they are doing reasonably well is on the moorland edges. Here pesticides are rarely used. Although the habitat is not always ideal and the climate can have an adverse effect on chick survival, effective predator control, so lacking on many lowland shoots, gives them the protection they need to survive. I hope so.

RECIPES

No book that tries to cover this subject would be complete without offering a few choice methods of enhancing the unsurpassed flavour of grouse for the table. I am grateful to those that have let me use their recipes and hope that you enjoy them too.

If you have some old grouse I highly recommend this recipe from Lady Claire Macdonald.

Grouse pudding with lemon crust
Serves 6

For the suet crust:

12 oz/340g self raising flour

6oz /170g shredded suet

Grated rind of one well washed and dried lemon

Salt and pepper

For the filling:

1 1/2 lb/675g old grouse, cut the meat off the carcase and cut into neat pieces as nearly equal in size as possible

2 tbsp flour

Salt and pepper

1 onion, skinned and chopped finely and neatly

1 pt/570ml water and red wine or port - I leave the ratio up to you

1 tbsp redcurrant jelly

Mix together the pastry ingredients and stir in enough cold water to mix to a dough - about 1/4pt/140ml. Roll out two-thirds of the dough and line a large pudding bowl with it - a boilable plastic bowl with a snap on lid is the ideal - capacity 3pts/1.7 litres. The pastry won't fill it.

Mix together the grouse, flour, seasoning and chopped onion. Pack this into the pastry-lined bowl. Measure half the water and wine (or port) into a small saucepan and stir in the redcurrant jelly. Heat until the jelly dissolves, then mix it with the rest of the liquid and pour this into the grouse mixture.

Roll out the remaining pastry into a circle to fit on the top of the grouse. Cut a circle of baking parchment to fit on top, making a small pleat in the middle of its diameter. Snap on the lid and put the bowl in a large pan with water coming halfway up the sides of the bowl. Cover the pan with a lid, and bring the water in the pan to a gently simmering point. Cook like this, with the water barely simmering, for 3 1/2 hours - 4 hours. Check the level of the water from time to time.

To reheat, steam for a further 2 hours. If you intend to serve the pudding after one steaming, steam for 5 hours.

Have a jug of hot water or stock to hand - game consomme is the best for this - to top up the liquid level inside the pudding as you spoon out the contents.

Annie May, whose husband Richard is trying to restore grouse to a small moor in Cheshire, is looking forward to trying this recipe on the first grouse shot on the moor.

Grouse with red onion marmalade
Serves 2

1 brace of grouse

3 large red onions

Olive oil

1 small glass red wine

1 15ml tbsp rowanberry jelly

Bacon

Salt and pepper

1 large heavy based frying pan with lid

Cover the base of the pan with olive oil. When it is nice and hot place the grouse, breasts down, in the pan. Cover and cook for about 5 minutes shaking the pan to prevent burning. Remove grouse, cover with strips of bacon and place in Aga roasting tin in the bottom of the moderately hot (190C/375F/Gas5) top roasting oven, for 20/25 minutes.

Put chopped red onions in frying pan, add a drizzle of extra virgin olive oil, cover and fry gently until soft - do not let them brown. Add red wine and rowanberry jelly, salt and pepper to taste, cover and simmer for 10 - 15 minutes. Taste and adjust the seasoning. Remove grouse to serving plate with the bacon snipped over. Add grouse juices to red onion mixture. Serve grouse with the onion marmalade, game chips and fresh vegetables.

Sadly my freezer is bereft of grouse so I will have to wait until August before trying this mouth watering recipe from John Burton-Race, of the Landmark Hotel, London NW1, who has recently been awarded two Michelin stars.

Grouse as in Yorkshire
Serves 8

8 young grouse

5 1/4 pts/3 litres of chicken stock

7 fl oz/200 ml of red wine vinegar

1 bottle of Denbies 1990 Dornfelder, or any good medium bodied red wine such as a Côtes du Rhône

3 1/2 fl oz/100 ml of Port

2 tsp of redcurrent jelly

8 juniper berries

1 sprig thyme, 1 bay leaf

1 onion, 1/2 carrot, 6 shallots

1 leek, 1/2 stick celery

4 cloves of garlic

16 rashers of smoked streaky bacon

Salt and pepper

1 oz/30 g of butter

Cooking oil

1 oz/30 g chopped liver

Singe all the grouse and remove breast bones. Season with salt and pepper and tie two rashers of bacon either side of the breast lighly with string. Heat a large roasting tray and lightly oil. Seal the grouse on either side until golden brown. Set to roast in a medium to hot oven turning the grouse from one side to the other after six minutes and finally finishing on the back for five more minutes. Remove from the oven, cut off the string and bacon, brown the breast skin in the hot pan then allow the grouse to rest.

Bone the grouse, taking the legs off in one piece and also the breast. Bone out the thigh bone and clean around the drumstick, pulling out any tendons showing. Trim the breast being careful to remove any darkened part which has been near the chest cavity as this can be very bitter and unpleasant.

Keep prepared meat warm aside covered with a butter paper and roughly chop the carcasses. In the same roasting pan brown off the bones and the chopped vegetables. Remove with a slotted spoon, tip off any excess fat and deglaze with red wine vinegar. Boil rapidly scraping off any sediment and add the redcurrent jelly and crushed juniper. Allow to get sticky then put back the bones stirring them over and over all the time so as not to let them burn. When nicely glazed, remove to a tall pan and deglaze again with the red wine. Flambe and reduce by half or until the right degree of acidity has been obtained. Add the port, boil and add to the bones. Cover with chicken stock, put in the thyme, bay leaf and garlic, bring to the boil and skim. Simmer for ten to fifteen minutes, no longer or the sauce can become bitter.

Strain and set to reduce over a high flame, skimming all the while. At this stage a tablespoon of meat glaze can be added.

As the sauce is nearing completion, re-heat the grouse. Pass the sauce through a muslin cloth to trap all the blood particles. Bring back to the boil and taste. If the sauce is too strong a drop of cream can be added but it tends to make the final result cloudy. Having seasoned the sauce, at the last minute whisk in the butter and chopped liver.

Assemble the grouse on a large plate and garnish with fresh baby brussel sprouts, game chips and salsify.

Spoon over the hot sauce onto the dressed plates.